READ WELL®

Mammal Pets

Teacher's Guide

Read Well 1 · Unit 12

Cc

C says /c/.
Quick Sound (not cuh)
Unvoiced/Quiet

Critical Foundations in Primary Reading

Marilyn Sprick, Lisa Howard, Ann Fidanque, Shelley V. Jones

Copyright 2007 (Second Edition) Sopris West Educational Services. All rights reserved.

ISBN 13-digit: 978-1-59318-410-0   ISBN 10-digit: 1-59318-410-7   131844/4-13

12 13 14 15 16 RRDHRBVA 17 16 15 14 13

Cambium LEARNING® Group | **Voyager** LEARNING

Table of Contents
Unit 12
Mammal Pets

I I Voiced (Word) **Unit A**	**Mm** /mmm/ **Monkey** Continuous Voiced **Unit B**	**Ss** /sss/ **Snake** Continuous Unvoiced **Unit 1**	**Ee** /eee/ **Emu** Continuous Voiced (Long) **Unit 2**	**ee** /eeee/ **Bee** Continuous Voiced (Long) **Unit 2**	**Mm** /mmm/ **Monkey** Continuous Voiced **Unit 3**
Aa /aaa/ **Ant** Continuous Voiced (Short) **Unit 4**	**Dd** /d/ **Dinosaur** Quick Voiced (not duh) **Unit 5**	**th** /ththth/ **the** Continuous Voiced **Unit 6**	**Nn** /nnn/ **Nest** Continuous Voiced **Unit 7**	**Tt** /t/ **Turkey** Quick Unvoiced (not tuh) **Unit 8**	**Ww** /www/ **Wind** Continuous Unvoiced (woo) **Unit 9**
Ii /iii/ **Insects** Continuous Voiced (Short) **Unit 10**	**Th** /Ththth/ **The** Continuous Voiced **Unit 10**	**Hh** /h/ **Hippo** Quick Unvoiced (not huh) **Unit 11**	**Cc** /c/ **Cat** Quick Unvoiced (not cuh) **Unit 12**	**Rr** /rrr/ **Rabbit** Continuous Voiced **Unit 13**	**ea** /eaeaea/ **Eagle** Continuous Voiced (Long) **Unit 13**
Sh/sh /shshsh/ **Sheep** Continuous Unvoiced **Unit 14**	**Kk, -ck** /k/ **Kangaroo** Quick Unvoiced (not kuh) **Unit 15**	**oo** /oooo/ **Moon** Continuous Voiced (Long) **Unit 16**	**ar** /ar/ **Shark** Voiced (R-Controlled) **Unit 17**	**Wh/wh** /wh/ **Whale** Quick Voiced **Unit 18**	**Ee** /ĕĕĕ/ **Engine or Ed** Continuous Voiced (Short) **Unit 19**
-y /-yyy/ **Fly** Continuous Voiced (Long) **Unit 20**	**Ll** /lll/ **Letter** Continuous Voiced **Unit 21**	**Oo** /ooo/ **Otter** Continuous Voiced (Short) **Unit 22**	**Bb** /b/ **Bat** Quick Voiced (not buh) **Unit 23**	**all** /all/ **Ball** Voiced **Unit 23**	**Gg** /g/ **Gorilla** Quick Voiced (not guh) **Unit 24**
Ff /fff/ **Frog** Continuous Unvoiced **Unit 25**	**Uu** /uuu/ **Umbrella** Continuous Voiced (Short) **Unit 26**	**er** /er/ **Sister** Voiced (R-Controlled) **Unit 27**	**oo** /oo/ **Book** Voiced (Short) **Unit 27**	**Yy** /y-/ **Yarn** Quick Voiced **Unit 28**	**Aa** /a/ **Ago** Voiced (Schwa) **Unit 28**
Pp /p/ **Pig** Quick Unvoiced (not puh) **Unit 29**	**ay** /ay/ **Hay** Voiced **Unit 29**	**Vv** /vvv/ **Volcano** Continuous Voiced **Unit 30**	**Qu/qu** /qu/ **Quake** Quick Unvoiced **Unit 31**	**Jj** /j/ **Jaguar** Quick Voiced (not juh) **Unit 32**	**Xx** /ksss/ **Fox** Continuous Unvoiced **Unit 33**
or /or/ **Horn** Voiced (R-Controlled) **Unit 33**	**Zz** /zzz/ **Zebra** Continuous Voiced **Unit 34**	**a_e** /a_e/ **Cake** Bossy E Voiced (Long) **Unit 34**	**-y** /-y/ **Baby** Voiced **Unit 35**	**i_e** /i_e/ **Kite** Bossy E Voiced (Long) **Unit 35**	**ou** /ou/ **Cloud** Voiced **Unit 36**
ow /ow/ **Cow** Voiced **Unit 36**	**Ch/ch** /ch/ **Chicken** Quick Unvoiced **Unit 37**	**ai** /ai/ **Rain** Voiced (Long) **Unit 37**	**igh** /igh/ **Flight** Voiced (Long) **Unit 38**	**o_e** /o_e/ **Bone** Bossy E Voiced (Long) **Unit 38**	**ir** /ir/ **Bird** Voiced (R-Controlled) **Unit 38**

Introduction
Mammal Pets

Story Notes

In Unit 12, children review the facts they know about mammals, and apply that knowledge to two of our favorite pets—cats and dogs. Then children read a gentle story about an old woman who learns that feeding and caring for an animal has its rewards.

Recommended Read Aloud

For reading outside of small group instruction

Millions of Cats by Wanda Ga'g

Fiction • Narrative

An old favorite, *Millions of Cats* is the classic tale of an old man and woman who go in search of a cat. To their surprise, they encounter hundreds, and thousands, and millions of cats!

Read Well Connection

In Unit 12, children encounter old Miss Tam. Unlike the old man and woman who go looking for a cat, Miss Tam likes her peace and quiet. However, like the old man and woman, Miss Tam finds that even an old and scraggly cat can be a comforting companion.

NOTE FROM THE AUTHORS

Practice makes perfect. The old adage applies to reading instruction. Thankfully, young children love to hear and read the same story over and over again. Be creative in the ways you encourage children to do repeated readings of their Solo and Homework Stories. Have them practice for a tape-recorded reading! Have them read into a karaoke machine. Share your ideas with colleagues.

New and Important Objectives
A Research-Based Reading Program
Just Right for Young Children

Oral Language
Phonemic Awareness
Phonics
Fluency
Vocabulary
Comprehension

◆◆ **Oral Language**

Language patterns can be found in Stretch and Shrink, Smooth and Bumpy Blending, Sounding Out Smoothly, and Dictation. Continue practice throughout the day. Prompt students who would benefit from additional oral language practice to use the language patterns during instruction. (See page 10 for a list of the Unit 12 Oral Language Patterns.)

Phonemic Awareness

Isolating Beginning, Middle, Ending Sounds, Segmenting, Blending, Manipulating, Rhyming, Onset and Rime

Phonics

Letter Sounds and Combinations
   ☆ Cc
   ☆ sc-
   Review • Ss, Ee, ee, Mm, Aa, Dd, th, Nn, Tt, Ww, Ii, Th, Hh

Pattern Words
   ☆can, ☆can't, ☆Cass, ☆cat, ☆Cats, ☆cat's, ☆deeds, ☆didn't, ☆hadn't, ☆Hats, ☆heeds, ☆hiss, ☆Hiss, ☆hit, ☆miss, ☆Miss, ☆Nat's, ☆scat, ☆Swiss, ☆Tee hee, ☆That's
   Review • am, an, and, ant, did, dim, had, hat, He, hid, him, in, it, mad, me, Me, Meet, mist, needs, sad, Sam, sat, Scat, see, See, seeds, seem, seen, sit, sweet, teen, that, That, This, Tim, tin, We, weeds, win

Tricky Words
   ☆a, ☆hasn't, ☆isn't, ☆wasn't
   Review • as, has, his, His, I, is, said, the, The, was, with

C says /c/.
Curious cat,
/C/, /c/, /c/.

Quick Sound (not cuh)

◆◆ = Oral language patterns   ☆ = New in this unit

2

Comprehension

Comprehension Strategies

Building Knowledge, Priming Background Knowledge, Making Connections, Predicting, Identifying, Describing, Demonstrating, Explaining, Inferring, Responding, Visualizing, Summarizing, Sequencing

Story Elements

Title, Who (Character), Where (Setting), What (Action)

Story Vocabulary

★Cat, ★Dog, ★Skeleton

Text Structure

Beginning, Middle, End

Expository Elements

Topic, Fact

Genre

Nonfiction • Expository

Fiction • Narrative

Lessons

★Feeding and caring for an animal has its rewards.

★Old facts help you learn about new things.

Written Response

Sentence Copying, Sentence Illustration, Sentence Completion, Sentence Comprehension—Multiple Choice

Fluency

Accuracy, Expression, Rate

Daily Lesson Planning

PACING

Some students will begin the process of learning to read slowly but make rapid progress later. To be at grade level by the end of the year, first graders need to complete Unit 20 by the end of the 18th week of school. Groups that are working at a slower pace may require more intensive *Read Well* instruction and practice. (See *Getting Started: A Guide to Implementation.*)

ASSESSMENT

Upon completion of this unit, assess each student and proceed to Unit 13 as appropriate.

SAMPLE LESSON PLANS

The sample lesson plans illustrate how materials can be used for students with different learning needs. Each lesson plan is designed to provide daily decoding practice and story reading.

A BASIC RULE (Reminder)
Make adjustments frequently, moving students as quickly as possible without sacrificing mastery.

2-DAY PLAN • *Acceleration*

Day 1	**Day 2**
• Decoding Practice 1	• Decoding Practice 2
• Stories 3 and 4	• Stories 5 and 6 and Story Summary
• Skill Work 3*	• Skill Work 5*
• Comprehension Work 4*	• Skill Work 6*
• Homework 1, Story 2*	• Homework 3, Story 6*
• Homework 2, Story 4*	• Homework 4, Storybook Decoding Review*

In this 2-Day Plan students skip Decoding Practice 3, Decoding Practice 4, and Stories 1 and 2. (Story 2 may be used as homework.)

With this lesson plan, you will need to introduce "scat," "Miss," and "wasn't" to students on Day 1 (before they read Stories 3 and 4), and introduce "hasn't" before they read Stories 5 and 6.

3-DAY PLAN

Day 1	**Day 2**	**Day 3**
• Decoding Practice 1	• Decoding Practice 2	• Decoding Practice 3
• Story 1, Fact Summary, and Story 2	• Stories 3 and 4	• Stories 5 and 6 and Story Summary
• Skill Work 1*	• Skill Work 3*	• Skill Work 5*
• Comprehension Work 2*	• Comprehension Work 4*	• Skill Work 6*
• Homework 1, Story 2*	• Homework 2, Story 4*	• Homework 3, Story 6*
		• Homework 4, Storybook Decoding Review*

4-DAY PLAN

Day 1	**Day 2**	**Day 3**	**Day 4**
• Decoding Practice 1	• Decoding Practice 2	• Decoding Practice 3	• Decoding Practice 4
• Story 1, Fact Summary, and Story 2	• Stories 3 and 4	• Stories 5 and 6 and Story Summary	• Review Stories 2, 4, and 6
• Skill Work 1*	• Skill Work 3*	• Skill Work 5*	• Skill Work 6*
• Comprehension Work 2*	• Comprehension Work 4*	• Homework 3, Story 6*	• Homework 4, Storybook Decoding Review*
• Homework 1, Story 2*	• Homework 2, Story 4*		

4   * From *Read Well* Comprehension and Skill Work (workbook), *Read Well* Homework (blackline masters), or Extra Practice in this book.

6-DAY PLAN • *Pre-Intervention*

Day 1	Day 2	Day 3
• Decoding Practice 1 • Story 1 and Fact Summary • Skill Work 1*	• Review Decoding Practice 1 • Story 2 • Comprehension Work 2* • Homework 1, Story 2*	• Decoding Practice 2 • Story 3 • Skill Work 3*
Day 4	**Day 5**	**Day 6**
• Review Decoding Practice 2 • Story 4 • Comprehension Work 4* • Homework 2, Story 4*	• Decoding Practice 3 • Story 5 • Skill Work 5* • Homework 4, Storybook Decoding Review*	• Decoding Practice 4 • Story 6 and Story Summary • Skill Work 6* • Homework 3, Story 6*

PRE-INTERVENTION AND INTERVENTION

See *Getting Started: A Guide to Implementation* for information on how to achieve mastery at a faster pace with students who require six or more days of instruction.

8-DAY PLAN • *Intervention*

Day 1	Day 2	Day 3	Day 4
• Decoding Practice 1 • Story 1 and Fact Summary • Skill Work 1*	• Review Decoding Practice 1 • Story 2 • Comprehension Work 2* • Homework 1, Story 2*	• Decoding Practice 2 • Story 3 • Skill Work 3*	• Review Decoding Practice 2 • Story 4 • Comprehension Work 4* • Homework 2, Story 4*
Day 5	**Day 6**	**Day 7**	**Day 8**
• Decoding Practice 3 • Story 5 • Skill Work 5* • Homework 4, Storybook Decoding Review*	• Decoding Practice 4 • Story 6 and Story Summary • Skill Work 6* • Homework 3, Story 6*	• Extra Practice 1* • Extra Practice Activity 1*	• Extra Practice 2* • Extra Practice Activity 2*

10-DAY PLAN • *Intervention*

Day 1	Day 2	Day 3	Day 4	Day 5
• Decoding Practice 1 • Story 1 and Fact Summary • Skill Work 1*	• Review Decoding Practice 1 • Story 2 • Comprehension Work 2* • Homework 1, Story 2*	• Decoding Practice 2 • Story 3 • Skill Work 3*	• Review Decoding Practice 2 • Story 4 • Comprehension Work 4* • Homework 2, Story 4*	• Decoding Practice 3 • Story 5 • Skill Work 5* • Homework 4, Storybook Decoding Review*
Day 6	**Day 7**	**Day 8**	**Day 9**	**Day 10**
• Decoding Practice 4 • Story 6 and Story Summary • Skill Work 6* • Homework 3, Story 6*	• Extra Practice 1* • Extra Practice Activity 1*	• Extra Practice 2* • Extra Practice Activity 2*	• Extra Practice 3 • Storybook Decoding Review • Review Solos: Units 9 and 10** • Extra Practice Activity 3*	• Extra Practice 4 • Review Decoding Practice 4 • Review Solos: Units 11 and 12** • Extra Practice Activity 4*

** Use review stories as listed or substitute with stories from *Read Well K*, Unit 12.

Materials and Materials Preparation

Core Lessons

Teacher Materials

READ WELL MATERIALS

- Unit 12 Teacher's Guide
- Sound and Word Cards for Units 1–12
- Smooth and Bumpy Blending Cards 22, 23, 24, 25
- Spring toys (optional for use with Stretch and Shrink)
- Game markers (optional for use with cover-up activities)
- *Assessment Manual* or page 56

SCHOOL SUPPLIES

- Stopwatch or watch with second hand

Student Materials

READ WELL MATERIALS

- Decoding Book 2 for each student
- Unit 12 Storybook for each student
- Unit 12 Comprehension and Skill Work for each student (My Activity Book 2)
- Unit 12 Certificate of Achievement (blackline master page 57)
- Unit 12 Homework for each student (blackline masters)
  See *Getting Started* for suggested homework routines.

SCHOOL SUPPLIES

- Pencils, colors (optional—markers, crayons, or colored pencils)

Make one copy per student of each blackline master as appropriate for the group.

Note: For new or difficult Comprehension and Skill Work activities, make overhead transparencies from the blackline masters. Use the transparencies to demonstrate and guide practice.

Extra Practice Lessons

Note: Use these lessons only if needed.

Student Materials

READ WELL MATERIALS

- Unit 12 Extra Practice 1 and 2 for each student (blackline master pages 59 and 63)
- Unit 12 Extra Practice Activities 1, 2, 3, and 4 for each student (blackline master pages 60–61 double-sided; 64; 66–67 single-sided; 68)

SCHOOL SUPPLIES

- Pencils, colors (markers, crayons, or colored pencils), highlighters, scissors, glue
- White boards or paper

Important Tips

In this section, you will find:

☆ Smooth and Bumpy Blending With <u>Cc</u>

/C/ is both quick and unvoiced, making blending difficult. A fully scripted lesson is provided on page 8 so you can study, rehearse, and visualize how to teach this skill—prior to working with children.

☆ Jell-Well Reviews

When children enter school with little or no literacy background, or are among the few children for whom learning to read is very difficult, a periodic review of earlier units is sometimes necessary.

☆ Language Priming—Using "Not"

Use the information on page 10 to encourage English Language Learners (ELL students) and children with language delays to use the language patterns provided in *Read Well*. This lesson reviews and extends the use of negatives.

★Smooth and Bumpy Blending With <u>Cc</u>

PRONUNCIATION

The letter <u>Cc</u> is both a quick (or stop) sound and unvoiced. Teach students to say an unvoiced /c/, not /cuh/. The /cuh/ pronunciation makes word recognition unnecessarily difficult, e.g., /cuh-aaa-tuh/ vs. /caaat/.

BLENDING

Bumpy Blending prepares students for the more difficult Smooth Blending. With Smooth Blending, children are taught to pronounce /c/ and the adjoining vowel as one sound. With the word "cat" you will demonstrate and guide blending by looping directly to /aaa/. The whole word is blended in one continuous breath as follows: /caaat/.

BLENDING CARD 24

Use Blending Card 24 to teach students how to blend letter <u>c</u>.

- Demonstrate Bumpy Blending of *cat*.

    I'm going to do Bumpy Blending.

    Tap under each letter. /c/ • /a/ • /t/

    Tell me the word. (cat)

    What does a *cat* say? A cat says "meow."

- Guide Bumpy Blending of *cat*.

    Everyone, let's do Bumpy Blending together.

    Tap under each letter. /c/ • /a/ • /t/

- Repeat with group and individual turns, independent of your voice.

- Demonstrate Smooth Blending of *cat*.

    I'm going to do Smooth Blending.

    Loop to letter <u>a</u>, then to letter <u>t</u>. /caaat/

- Guide Smooth Blending of *cat*.

    Let's do Smooth Blending together.

    Loop to letter <u>a</u>, then to letter <u>t</u>. /caaat/

    Say the word. (cat)

- Repeat with group and individual turns, independent of your voice.

BUILDING INDEPENDENCE

During the first day or two of instruction, demonstrate how to blend with /c/. By the second or third day of instruction, begin exercises with independent practice. If students have difficulty, diagnose the problem and precorrect using the following procedures.

★ Difficulty Blending Smoothly

- Have students identify whether you are doing Smooth or Bumpy Blending.

- Have students identify the vowel before blending smoothly.

Incorrect Sound

Identify the difficult sound first, then sound it out.

★ Jell-Well Reviews

PURPOSE

All children begin learning to read with their own unique literacy history and predisposition for learning to read. For those who begin with fewer resources and skills, a periodic review is sometimes critical to moving forward. A "Jell-Well Review" is the *Read Well* version of this process. It is a period of time taken to celebrate what a group of children have learned, while cementing previously learned skills.

WHEN TO DO A JELL-WELL REVIEW

When a child or group of children receive a Weak Pass for two consecutive units, provide a Jell-Well Review. A brief intervention for an individual child can prevent the need for intensive remediation later. A Jell-Well Review for a group can allow more rapid progress through later units.

PROCEDURES

Determine when the individual child or the group last received Strong Passes (or 100% accuracy in Units 1–4). Go back to this unit and proceed forward again—as rapidly as possible. Develop Jell-Well Lessons that include, on a daily basis:

- Sound and Word Card Practice
  Read Well students rarely have difficulty with sounds.
  If students have consistently scored 100% on Subtest A,
  review all known sounds to date. (For example, if the
  group is in Unit 12 and begins a Jell-Well Review at Unit 8,
  continue to review sounds through Unit 12 each day.)

- Stretch and Shrink
  Select two or three words from Word Practice. (See below.)
  Have students use spring toys as they Stretch and Shrink words.
  Include individual turns so you can assess individual progress.

- Blending Card Practice
  Review cards listed in the review unit.

- Word Practice
  Have students work on Decoding Practice 4 and the Extra
  Practice Blackline Masters from the review unit.

- Solo Story Reading With Repeated Readings
  Provide daily repeated readings of Solo Stories from the review
  unit. Homework Blackline Masters and Extra Practice provide
  excellent resources. (Some teachers copy the Homework
  Blackline Masters to create Solo Story notebooks.)

LESSON PLANNER

A Jell-Well Review Planner and more detailed information can be found in *Getting Started: A Guide to Implementation* and in the *Assessment Manual*.

⭐Language Priming—Using "Not"
For English Language Learners and Children With Language Delays

With this sample lesson, children review and extend oral language practice with positive and negative statements.

EXAMPLE: Students review the question/response pattern:
Look at the picture. Is that a [dog]? (No, that is not a [dog].)
Look at the picture. Is that a [dog]? (Yes, that is a [dog].)

Use pictures from books and/or objects that students need to know.

[Ahmed], look at the picture. Is that a [book]? (No)

Say the whole sentence "No, that is not a [book]."
(No, that is not a [book].)

When the opportunity arises, make a conscious effort to use the sentences.

[Ahmed], look outside. Is that a [dog]? (No)

Say the whole sentence "No, that is not a [dog]."
(No, that is not a [dog].)

Repeating language patterns are marked with ◆◆s throughout the Teacher's Guide.

ORAL LANGUAGE PATTERNS	
Introduced in This Unit and Reviewed From Previous Units	
⭐What can the *cats* do? (They can [sing].)	⭐Whose hat is it? (The *cat's*)
⭐*Cass* is someone's name. Are you *Cass*? ([No])	⭐The cat just woke up. He *isn't* tired.
⭐An animal with antlers is a *deer*.	⭐The boy had a big lunch. He *wasn't* hungry.
⭐What do you *hear*? (I hear [music].)	⭐That hungry cat *hasn't* had his dinner.
⭐The bear is up in the . . . (tree).	What does a *cat* say? (A *cat* says "meow.")
⭐Show me *three* fingers.	What *can* we do? (We can [read].)
⭐[Brenda] *has* a [watch]. What does [Brenda] have?	Yesterday, we *had* . . . [fun].
⭐The man said, "Go away! *Scat!*" What did he say? (*Scat*)	See [Sam] and *his* [dog].
⭐*Miss* Tam has an old tomcat. Who has a tomcat? (*Miss* Tam)	What is this? (This is *an* [apple].)
⭐*Tam* is a name. Are you *Tam*? ([No])	Tiny drops of rain are called *mist*.
⭐That's *Nat's* [desk]. Whose [desk] is that? (*Nat's*)	Look at [Julian]. What is *he* doing? (*He* is [reading].)
⭐How many *hats* do you have? (I have [two] *hats*.)	Look at [Dillon]. See *him* [read].
⭐After [reading], we do . . . (*math*).	What is *this*? (*This* is a [pencil].)
⭐Who do you go to school *with*? (I go to school *with* [my friends].)	What do you do with *weeds*? (Pull them.)

⭐ = New in this unit

How to Teach the Lessons

Teach from this section. Each instructional component is outlined in an easy-to-teach format. Special tips are provided to help you nurture student progress.

In this section, you will find:

Decoding Practice 1
- Unit Introduction
- Story 1, Duet
- Fact Summary
- Skill Work Activity 1
- Story 2, Solo
- Comprehension Work Activity 2

Decoding Practice 2
- Story 3, Duet
- Skill Work Activity 3
- Story 4, Solo
- Comprehension Work Activity 4

Decoding Practice 3
- Story 5, Duet
- Skill Work Activity 5
- Story 6, Solo
- Story Summary
- Skill Work Activity 6

Decoding Practice 4
Review Solo Stories

SCAFFOLDED INSTRUCTION
Developmental Shift

As children gain confidence across units, begin with guided practice or independent practice, as appropriate.

If a new word is difficult, you may wish to begin with a demonstration and guided practice.

11

❶ SOUND REVIEW

❷ NEW SOUND INTRODUCTION

❸ NEW SOUND PRACTICE

◆◆ ❹ STRETCH AND SHRINK

cats-caaatsss-cats	What can the *cats* do? (They can [sing].)
Cass-Caaassss-Cass	*Cass* is someone's name. Are you *Cass*? ([No])
deer-deeeerrr-deer	An animal with antlers is a *deer*.
hear-heaeaearrr-hear	What do you *hear*? (I *hear* [music].)

◆◆ ❺ SMOOTH AND BUMPY BLENDING—CARDS 24, 25

◆◆ ❻ SOUNDING OUT SMOOTHLY

For each word, have students blend /C/ with the vowel first, sound out the word, and then read the word: caaa-caaannn-can; caaa-caaat-cat; Caaa-Caaassss-Cass.
Use the words in sentences as needed.

✿	*caaannn-can*	What *can* we do? (We *can* [read].)
	caaat-cat	What does a *cat* say? (A *cat* says "meow.")
	Caaassss-Cass	*Cass* is someone's name. Are you *Cass*? ([No])
♥	*haaad-had*	Yesterday, we *had* . . . [fun].
	mmmiiissst-mist	Tiny drops of rain are called *mist*.
●	*Heee-He*	Look at [Julian]. What is *he* doing? (*He* is [reading].)
	aaannn-an	What is this? (This is *an* [apple].)

◆◆ ❼ POSSESSIVE 'S

• Have students sound out "cat's" smoothly, ignoring the apostrophe. Say something like:
  Remember, you sound out words with the little mark called an apostrophe.
  Read the first word. (The)
  Let's sound out the next words, then read them. /caaatsss/, cat's, /haaat/, hat
  Let's read the phrase. The cat's hat
  The apostrophe tells us something belongs to the cat. Whose hat is it? (The cat's)
• Repeat practice. Mix group and individual turns, independent of your voice.

❽ TRICKY WORDS

★ **New word: "a"**
To introduce the new word "a," say something like:
Look at the last Tricky Word. It is just the letter a. When you see the letter a in a sentence it says "a."
I see *a* [book]. What do you see? (I see *a* [book].) Say "a" five times.

❾ DAILY STORY READING

Proceed to the Unit 12 Storybook. See Daily Lesson Planning for pacing suggestions.

❿ COMPREHENSION AND SKILL WORK ACTIVITY 1 AND/OR ACTIVITY 2

See pages 21 and/or 25.

UNIT 12 DECODING PRACTICE 1
(For use with Stories 1 and 2)

1. SOUND REVIEW Use Sound Cards for Units 1–11.

2. NEW SOUND INTRODUCTION Have students echo (repeat) the phrases. Do not have students read the poem.

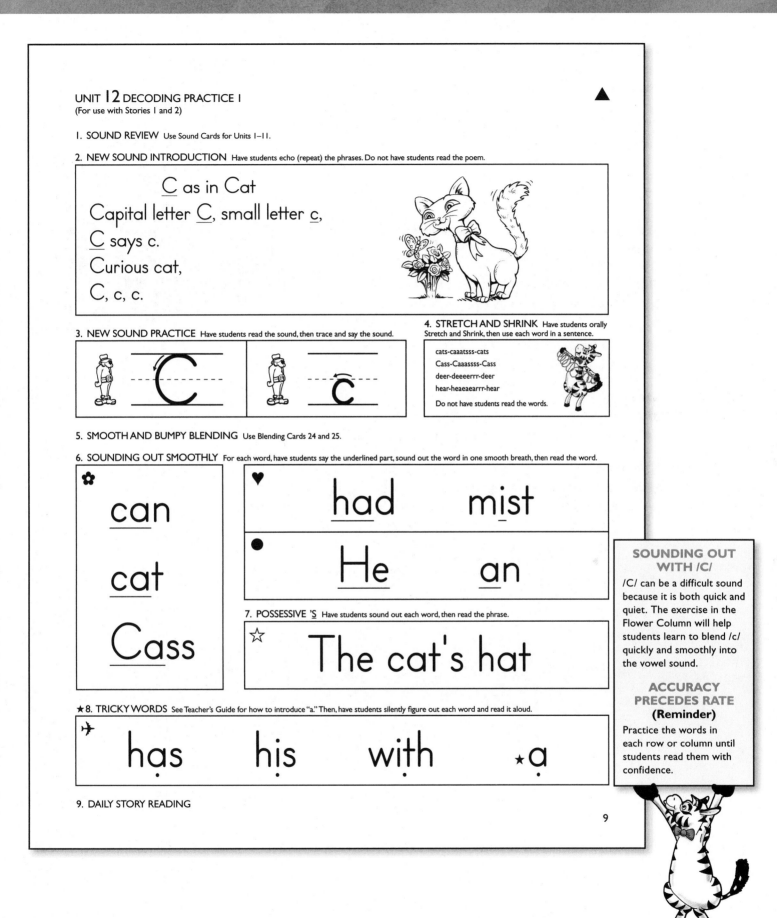

C as in Cat
Capital letter C, small letter c,
C says c.
Curious cat,
C, c, c.

3. NEW SOUND PRACTICE Have students read the sound, then trace and say the sound.

C   c

4. STRETCH AND SHRINK Have students orally Stretch and Shrink, then use each word in a sentence.

cats-caaatsss-cats
Cass-Caaassss-Cass
deer-deeeerrr-deer
hear-heaeaearrr-hear

Do not have students read the words.

5. SMOOTH AND BUMPY BLENDING Use Blending Cards 24 and 25.

6. SOUNDING OUT SMOOTHLY For each word, have students say the underlined part, sound out the word in one smooth breath, then read the word.

✿ can
cat
Cass

♥ had   mist

● He   an

7. POSSESSIVE 'S Have students sound out each word, then read the phrase.

☆ The cat's hat

★8. TRICKY WORDS See Teacher's Guide for how to introduce "a." Then, have students silently figure out each word and read it aloud.

✈ has   his   with   ★a

9. DAILY STORY READING

9

SOUNDING OUT
WITH /C/

/C/ can be a difficult sound because it is both quick and quiet. The exercise in the Flower Column will help students learn to blend /c/ quickly and smoothly into the vowel sound.

ACCURACY
PRECEDES RATE
(Reminder)

Practice the words in each row or column until students read them with confidence.

13

❶ INTRODUCING THE UNIT AND THE TITLE PAGE

Identifying—Title

Tell students the title of the unit is "Mammal Pets."

Teacher Think Aloud—Priming Background Knowledge

You're going to read about two mammals that people often have for pets.

You already know four facts about mammals.

Tell me the facts. (Mammals have a backbone. They have fur or hair. They breathe air. They take care of their babies.)

I think you already know some important facts about cats and dogs.

❷ INTRODUCING VOCABULARY

Vocabulary—Cat, Dog, Skeleton

Cat

Put your finger under the first picture of the cat.

A *cat* is a small, furry animal that purrs. Cats make good pets.

Dog

Put your finger under the next picture.

A *dog* is an animal that barks. Dogs make good pets.

Skeleton

Put your finger under the next picture.

A *skeleton* is the part of the body that is made up of bones.

Mammal Pets

By Marilyn Sprick
Illustrated by Page O'Rourke

Vocabulary Words

cat — A cat is a small, furry animal that purrs. Cats make good pets.

dog — A dog is an animal that barks. Dogs make good pets.

skeleton — A skeleton is the part of the body that is made up of bones.

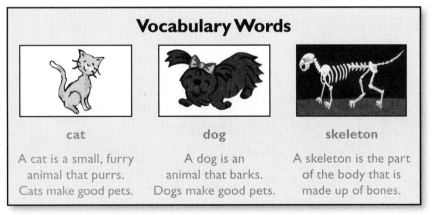

Vocabulary Words

cat
A cat is a small, furry animal that purrs. Cats make good pets.

dog
A dog is an animal that barks. Dogs make good pets.

skeleton
A skeleton is the part of the body that is made up of bones.

Defining Vocabulary—Cat, Dog, Skeleton

DUET STORY READING INSTRUCTIONS

Students read from their own storybooks.
The teacher reads the small text and students read the large text.

PACING

- 3- to 4-Day Plans: Have students do the first reading of Duet Story 1. Then proceed to repeated readings of Solo Story 2.
- 6- to 10-Day Plans: Have students do the first *and* second readings.

COMPREHENSION BUILDING:
DISCUSSION QUESTIONS AND TEACHER THINK ALOUDS

Ask questions and discuss text on the first or second reading when indicated in the storybook in light gray text.

PROCEDURES

1. First Reading

Have students identify the picture words {skeleton} and {nose}, then choral read the student text.

2. Second Reading

Have students take turns, with each student reading one line of student text.

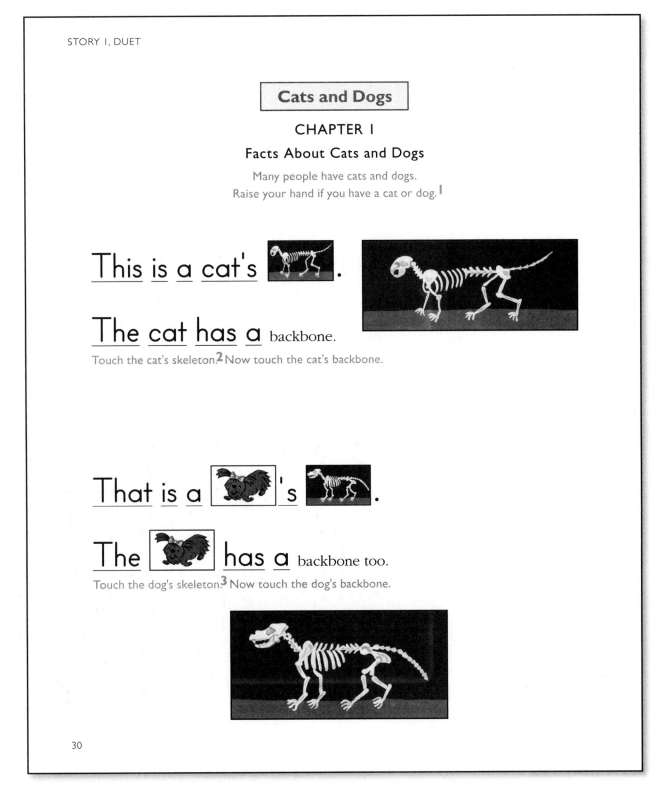

Cats and Dogs

CHAPTER 1

Facts About Cats and Dogs

Many people have cats and dogs.
Raise your hand if you have a cat or dog.[1]

This is a cat's ⬚ .

The cat has a backbone.

Touch the cat's skeleton.[2] Now touch the cat's backbone.

That is a ⬚'s ⬚ .

The ⬚ has a backbone too.

Touch the dog's skeleton.[3] Now touch the dog's backbone.

30

[1] **Making Connections**

[2] **Identifying, Using Vocabulary—Skeleton**

[3] **Identifying, Using Vocabulary—Skeleton**

A cat breathes air.

This is a cat.

See his 🐱.

That cat has a

very sensitive nose.

Cats have a better sense
of smell than people have.
A cat can tell who someone
is by smelling them.

What can a cat tell from smelling?[1](Who someone is)

Is a cat's sense of smell better than yours?[2](Yes)

A dog breathes air.

That 🐕 has a

very sensitive nose.

He can tell if an animal

is happy or mad by the animal's smell.

What can a dog tell from smelling an animal?[3](It can tell if the animal is happy or mad.)

Is a dog's sense of smell better than yours?[4](Yes)

31

❶ Identifying—Fact

❷ Identifying—Fact

❸ Identifying—Fact

❹ Inferring

STORY 1, DUET

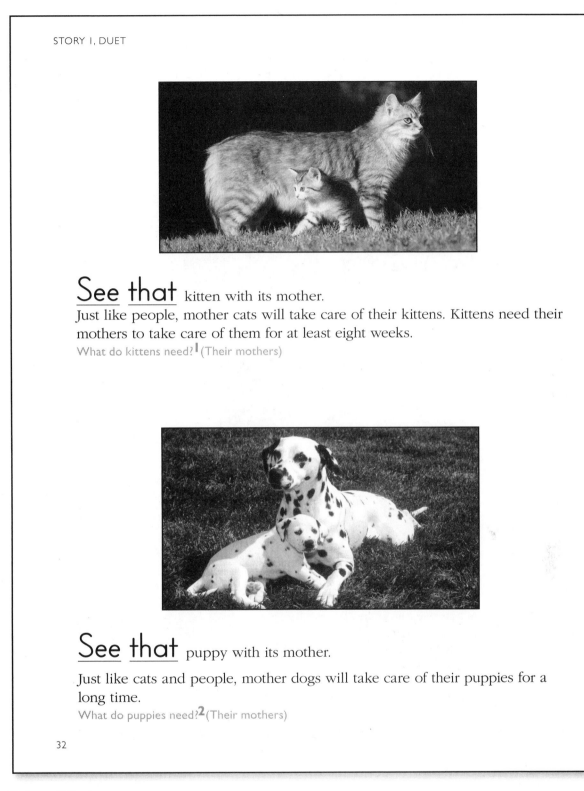

See that kitten with its mother.

Just like people, mother cats will take care of their kittens. Kittens need their mothers to take care of them for at least eight weeks.

What do kittens need?[1](Their mothers)

See that puppy with its mother.

Just like cats and people, mother dogs will take care of their puppies for a long time.

What do puppies need?[2](Their mothers)

32

❶ **Identifying—What**

❷ **Inferring**

COMPREHENSION BUILDING: FACT SUMMARY

Read the text and have students identify whether the animals are mammals or not as indicated by the procedures in light gray text. Children's mastery of facts is the food for higher order thinking. In this Fact Summary students conclude with an inductive thinking exercise.

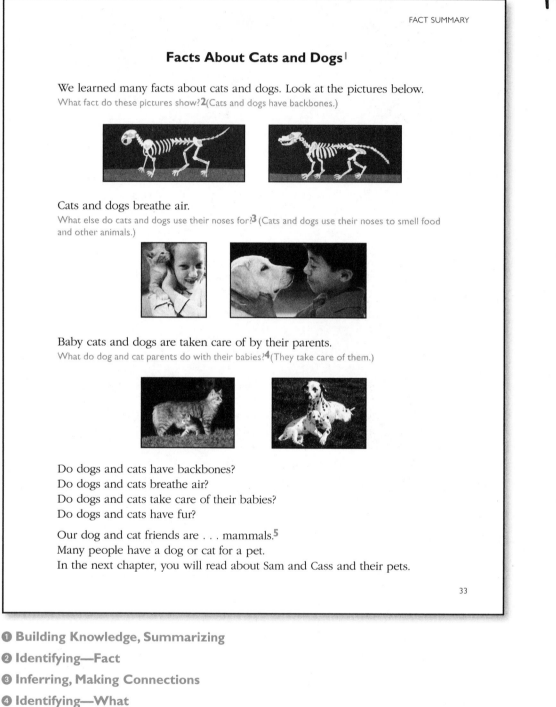

FACT SUMMARY

Facts About Cats and Dogs[1]

We learned many facts about cats and dogs. Look at the pictures below.

What fact do these pictures show?[2] (Cats and dogs have backbones.)

Cats and dogs breathe air.

What else do cats and dogs use their noses for?[3] (Cats and dogs use their noses to smell food and other animals.)

Baby cats and dogs are taken care of by their parents.

What do dog and cat parents do with their babies?[4] (They take care of them.)

Do dogs and cats have backbones?
Do dogs and cats breathe air?
Do dogs and cats take care of their babies?
Do dogs and cats have fur?

Our dog and cat friends are . . . mammals.[5]
Many people have a dog or cat for a pet.
In the next chapter, you will read about Sam and Cass and their pets.

33

❶ **Building Knowledge, Summarizing**

❷ **Identifying—Fact**

❸ **Inferring, Making Connections**

❹ **Identifying—What**

❺ **Classifying**

SOUND PAGE

Use work pages from the workbook.

PROCEDURES

For each step, demonstrate and guide practice as needed.

1. Handwriting—Basic Instructions
- Have students identify the capital letter <u>C</u> as in "Cat."
- Have students trace and write the capital letter <u>C</u>—leaving a finger space between each letter. Repeat with small letter <u>c</u> on the next two rows.

2. Drawing Pictures That Begin With /c/—Basic Instructions
- Have students brainstorm possible items.
  Examples: cat, camel, cake, carrot, candy cane, clown, cup, clock, crib . . .
- Have students fill the box with things that begin with /c/. Students can write the letter <u>c</u>, draw pictures of things that begin with /c/, cut out and paste up pictures of things that begin with /c/, or write words that begin with /c/.

Note: Neat work helps students take pride in their efforts.

SOLO STORY READING INSTRUCTIONS

Students read from their own storybooks.

COMPREHENSION BUILDING:
DISCUSSION QUESTIONS AND TEACHER THINK ALOUDS

Ask questions and discuss text on the first or second reading when indicated in the storybook in light gray text.

PROCEDURES

1. First Reading

Have students identify the picture words {dog} and {happy}, then choral read the text.

2. Second Reading

- Mix group and individual turns, independent of your voice. Have students work toward an accuracy goal of 0–2 errors. Quietly keep track of errors made by all students in each group.
- After reading the story, practice any difficult words.
- If the group has not reached the accuracy goal, have the group reread the story, mixing group and individual turns.

3. Repeated Readings
a. Timed Readings

- Once the accuracy goal has been achieved, have individual students read the page while the other children track the text with their fingers and whisper read.
  Time individuals for 30 seconds and encourage each student to work for his or her personal best.
- Count the number of words read correctly in 30 seconds (words read minus errors). Multiply by two to determine words read correctly per minute. Record student scores.

Note: Time students who are confident and enjoy the challenge. Accuracy precedes rate. If a student is unable to read with close to 100% accuracy, do not time the student. The personal goal should be accuracy. If the student is unable to read with accuracy, watch assessment results carefully. Evaluate group placement. Consider a Jell-Well Review.

b. Partner Reading

During students' daily independent work, have them do Partner Reading.

c. Homework 1

Have students read the story at home. (A reprint of this story is available on a blackline master in *Read Well* Homework.)

STORY 2, SOLO

CHAPTER 2

See the Cat and the

We see a cat and a [ ].

We see Cass with the [ ].

See Sam and his cat.

Who has a dog?[1] (Cass)
Who has a cat?[2] (Sam)

34

❶ Identifying—Who

❷ Identifying—Who

23

The cat needs Sam.

Sam and his cat seem 😃.

Why do you think the cat needs Sam?[1]

That 🐕 needs Cass.

Cass and the 🐕 seem 😃.

Why do you think the dog needs Cass?[2]

35

[1] Inferring

[2] Inferring

SENTENCE COMPREHENSION

Use work pages from the workbook.

CHECKOUT OPPORTUNITY

Listen to your students read individually while others work.

UNIT 12 COMPREHENSION WORK ACTIVITY 2 Name _____ ■
For use after Story 2

Sentence Comprehension

The cat needs Sam.

Sam and his cat seem [☺] .

Multiple Choice Identifying—Who →

1. The cat needs ____ .
   ○ Dad   ○ me   ● Sam

Multiple Choice Identifying—Who →

2. ____ and his cat seem [☺] .
   ○ Dad   ● Sam   ○ Dan

Writing, Complete Sentence →

Sentence Copying

The cat needs Sam.

The cat needs Sam.

14   © Sopris West Educational Services. All rights reserved.

PROCEDURES

For each step, demonstrate and guide practice as needed.

1. Sentence Comprehension—Basic Instructions
- Have students read the sentences at the top of the page.
- Have students read items 1 and 2, using the word "blank" when they see the line.
- Have students fill in the circle next to the correct word to fill in the blank.

2. Sentence Tracing and Copying—Basic Instructions
- Have students read and trace the sentence on the first line.
- Have students copy the sentence on the second line.

Note: You may wish to remind students that a sentence begins with a capital letter and ends with a period.

1 SOUND REVIEW

2 BEGINNING SOUND

◆◆ **3 STRETCH AND SHRINK**

tree-trrreeee-tree	The bear is up in the . . . (*tree*).
three-tbtbtbrrreeee-three	Show me *three* fingers.
his-biiizzz-his	See [Sam] and *his* [dog].
has-baaazzz-has	[Brenda] *has* a [watch]. What does [Brenda] have?

◆◆ **4 SMOOTH AND BUMPY BLENDING—CARDS 25, 23**

◆◆ **5 SOUNDING OUT SMOOTHLY**

★ **New blend: /sc-/,** ★ **New double consonant: ss**

For both the /sc-/ and the double consonant ss, have students sound out then say the underlined part. Next, have them sound out the word in one smooth breath, and then read the word. Use the words in sentences as needed.

✿	*caaat-cat*	What does a *cat* say? (A *cat* says "meow.")
	ssscaaat-scat	The man said, "Go away! *Scat*!" What did he say? (*Scat*)
	Tbtbtbiiisss-This	What is *this*? (*This* is a [pencil].)
♥	*Mmmiiissss-Miss*	*Miss* Tam has an old tomcat. Who has a tomcat? (*Miss* Tam)
	biiissss-hiss	What does a mad cat do? (*Hiss*)
	Taaammm-Tam	*Tam* is a name. Are you *Tam*? ([No])

6 ACCURACY AND FLUENCY BUILDING

★ **New contraction: n't**

These are students' first words with the contraction n't. Have them sound out the words. Use the words in sentences and then have students use the words in sentences.

• For each column, have students say the underlined part, then read each word.
• Have students read the whole column.
• Repeat practice on each column, building accuracy first and then fluency.

◆◆ **7 TRICKY WORDS**

★ **New words: "isn't" and "wasn't"**

• After students read "is," have them sound out their new word, "isn't."
  What small word do you see? (is) Let's sound out "isn't." /iiizzznnn't/
  Use the word in a sentence. The cat just woke up. He *isn't* tired.
• Have them read their new word three times.
• Repeat with "wasn't." Use the word in a sentence. The boy had a big lunch. He *wasn't* hungry.
• Repeat the row. Mix group and individual turns, independent of your voice.

8 DAILY STORY READING

Proceed to the Unit 12 Storybook. See Daily Lesson Planning for pacing suggestions.

9 COMPREHENSION AND SKILL WORK ACTIVITY 3 AND/OR ACTIVITY 4

See pages 33 and/or 37.

◆◆ For ELLs and children with language delays, provide repeated and extended practice with the language patterns. See page 10 for tips.

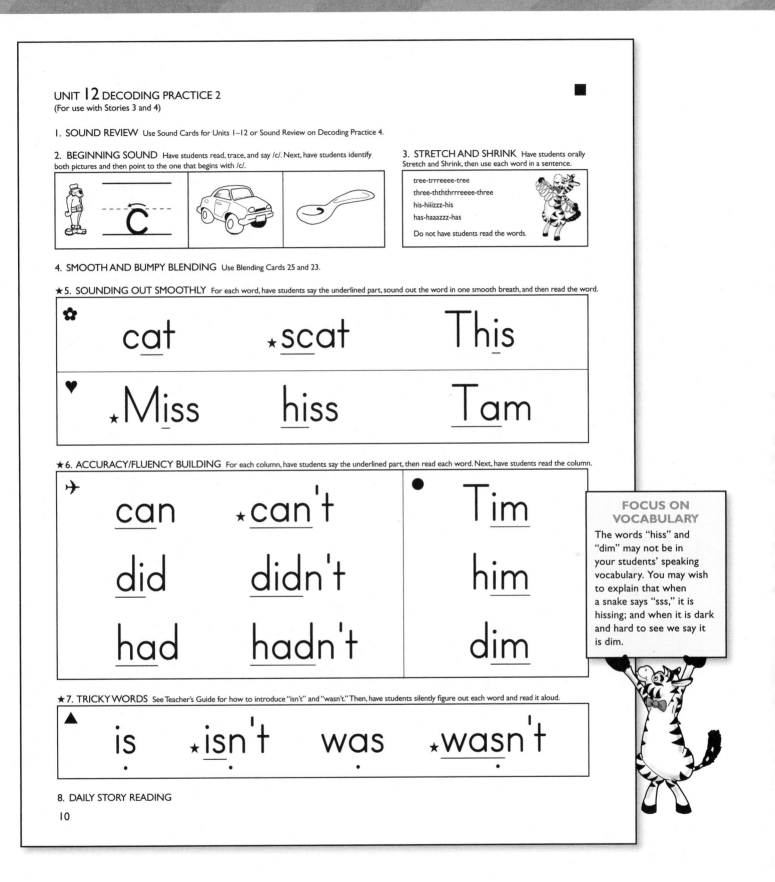

UNIT 12 DECODING PRACTICE 2
(For use with Stories 3 and 4)

1. SOUND REVIEW Use Sound Cards for Units 1–12 or Sound Review on Decoding Practice 4.

2. BEGINNING SOUND Have students read, trace, and say /c/. Next, have students identify both pictures and then point to the one that begins with /c/.

C

3. STRETCH AND SHRINK Have students orally Stretch and Shrink, then use each word in a sentence.

tree-trrreeee-tree
three-thththrrreeee-three
his-hiiizzz-his
has-haaazzz-has

Do not have students read the words.

4. SMOOTH AND BUMPY BLENDING Use Blending Cards 25 and 23.

★5. SOUNDING OUT SMOOTHLY For each word, have students say the underlined part, sound out the word in one smooth breath, and then read the word.

❀ c<u>a</u>t   ★sc<u>a</u>t   Thi<u>s</u>

♥ ★M<u>i</u>ss   h<u>i</u>ss   <u>T</u>am

★6. ACCURACY/FLUENCY BUILDING For each column, have students say the underlined part, then read each word. Next, have students read the column.

✈
<u>ca</u>n   ★<u>ca</u>n't   ● <u>T</u>im

<u>d</u>id   <u>d</u>idn't   <u>h</u>im

<u>h</u>ad   <u>h</u>adn't   <u>d</u>im

FOCUS ON VOCABULARY

The words "hiss" and "dim" may not be in your students' speaking vocabulary. You may wish to explain that when a snake says "sss," it is hissing; and when it is dark and hard to see we say it is dim.

★7. TRICKY WORDS See Teacher's Guide for how to introduce "isn't" and "wasn't." Then, have students silently figure out each word and read it aloud.

▲ <u>i</u>s   ★<u>i</u>sn't   <u>w</u>as   ★<u>w</u>asn't

8. DAILY STORY READING

10

27

DUET STORY READING INSTRUCTIONS

Students read from their own storybooks.

The teacher reads the small text and students read the large text.

PACING

- 2- to 4-Day Plans: Have students do the first reading of Duet Story 3.

  Then proceed to repeated readings of Solo Story 4.

- 6- to 10-Day Plans: Have students do the first *and* second readings.

COMPREHENSION BUILDING:
DISCUSSION QUESTIONS AND TEACHER THINK ALOUDS

Ask questions and discuss text on the first or second reading when indicated in the storybook in light gray text.

PROCEDURES

1. First Reading

Have students choral read the student text.

2. Second Reading

Have students take turns, with each student reading one line of student text.

Miss Tam's Cat

CHAPTER I

Miss Tam

Who do you think is going to be the main character? **I** (Miss Tam)

Meet Miss Tam.

Miss Tam was an old woman who lived in a big old house at the edge of town.

Miss Tam had a quaint and quiet life.

She planted seeds in her garden and watched the flowers grow.

Where did Miss Tam live? **2** (In a big old house at the edge of town)

What did Miss Tam do? **3** (Planted seeds and watched the flowers grow)

Miss Tam lived alone and liked it that way.

36

> **VISUALIZING, DESCRIBING**
>
> **After reading the page, say something like:** Look carefully at the picture. Who is the main character in this story? (Miss Tam)
>
> Now, close your eyes and imagine Miss Tam. What color is Miss Tam's hair? (Black)
>
> How old is she? (Very old)
>
> What does she like to do? (She likes to garden.)
>
> What else can you tell me about Miss Tam?

❶ Predicting

❷ Identifying—Where

❸ Identifying—Action

One day at half past two, a scruffy old tomcat appeared on Miss Tam's porch.

Miss Tam sat in her big old rocking chair reading a book.

"Hiss," said the cat.

Miss Tam was so surprised that she jumped ten feet up.

What did the cat do?**1** (The cat hissed and surprised Miss Tam.)
What did Miss Tam do?**2** (She jumped ten feet up.)

When she landed,

Miss Tam said, "Scat, cat!"

What do you think will happen next?**3**

FOCUS ON EXPRESSION

After reading the page, say something like:

Miss Tam wanted the cat to go away, so she said, "Scat, cat!" Do you think she said "Scat, cat" in a tiny little voice? (No)

Let's read the last sentence again. Remember to use a big voice for "Scat, cat."

37

❶ **Identifying—Action**
❷ **Identifying—Action**
❸ **Predicting**

The thin and lonely cat looked sad.

Miss Tam said, "Poor old cat."

Why did Miss Tam say "Poor old cat"?❚ (The cat looked sad, thin, and lonely.)

Miss Tam put her hand out for the cat to smell. He smelled her hand and rubbed against Miss Tam's leg. The old woman thought for a moment and said, "Okay, old fellow. Rest for a while." The cat purred; then he jumped right up into Miss Tam's lap! Before she knew it, Miss Tam found herself petting the ragged old tomcat.

38

❶ Inferring

The next day at half past five,

<u>Miss</u> <u>Tam</u> <u>sat</u> <u>in</u> her big old rocking chair reading a book

when the cat appeared again.

"<u>Hiss</u>," <u>said</u> <u>the</u> <u>cat.</u>

<u>Miss</u> <u>Tam</u> <u>was</u> so surprised that she jumped five feet up.

When she landed,

<u>Miss</u> <u>Tam</u> <u>said,</u> "<u>I</u> <u>said</u> <u>scat!</u>"

But then the cat smelled Miss Tam. She smelled familiar, so the cat began to purr. The old woman thought for a moment and said, "Okay, old fellow. Rest for a while."

At first, Miss Tam told the cat to . . .**1**(scat).

Did the cat scat or go away?**2**(No)

VISUALIZING, DESCRIBING

After reading the page, say something like: Look carefully at the picture. Now, close your eyes and imagine the cat. What color is the cat? (Gray)

What else can you tell me about the cat?

The cat purred and jumped right up into Miss Tam's lap. Before she knew it, Miss Tam found herself having dinner with the cat.

What did the cat do?**3**(The cat purred; the cat ate dinner with Miss Tam.)

39

❶ **Identifying**

❷ **Identifying**

❸ **Identifying—Action**

ALPHABET DETECTIVE
Use work pages from the workbook.

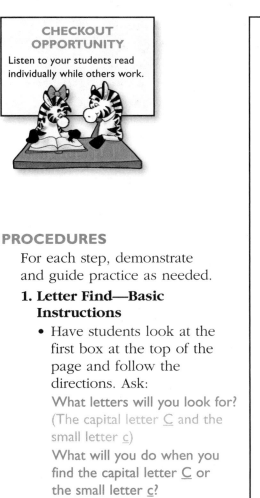

UNIT **12** SKILL WORK ACTIVITY 3   Name _____
ALPHABET DETECTIVE: For use after Story 3

C c   t

C as in Cat

Capital letter C, small letter c,

C says c.

Curious cat,

C, c, c.

15

PROCEDURES
For each step, demonstrate and guide practice as needed.

1. Letter Find—Basic Instructions

- Have students look at the first box at the top of the page and follow the directions. Ask:

  What letters will you look for? (The capital letter C and the small letter c)

  What will you do when you find the capital letter C or the small letter c? (Draw a square around it.)

- Have students look at the second box at the top of the page. Ask:

  What other letter will you look for? (The small letter t)

  What will you do when you find the small letter t? (Draw a circle around it.)

- Tell students to follow the directions in the first box for the whole poem; then follow the directions in the second box for the whole poem.

2. Self-Monitoring—Basic Instructions

Have students systematically check each line after finishing the task.

Alternative: At the beginning of the exercise, tell students the number of C's they will draw a square around, and the number of t's they will circle. Have students write the numbers on the top of their paper. When students complete the activity, have them count the number of circles and squares they have drawn. If the numbers are incorrect, they can recheck each line.

3. Coloring—Optional

Have students carefully color the picture, using at least three colors.

Note: If students have difficulty with the multi-step directions, have them do just the first step.

SOLO STORY READING INSTRUCTIONS

Students read from their own storybooks.

COMPREHENSION BUILDING:
DISCUSSION QUESTIONS AND TEACHER THINK ALOUDS

Ask questions and discuss text on the first or second reading when indicated in the storybook in light gray text.

PROCEDURES

1. First Reading

Have students identify the picture word {happy}, then choral read the text.

2. Second Reading

- Mix group and individual turns, independent of your voice. Have students work toward an accuracy goal of 0–2 errors. Quietly keep track of errors made by all students in each group.
- After reading the story, practice any difficult words.
- If the group has not reached the accuracy goal, have the group reread the story, mixing group and individual turns.

3. Repeated Readings

a. Timed Readings

- Once the accuracy goal has been achieved, have individual students read the page while the other children track the text with their fingers and whisper read.

  Time individuals for 30 seconds and encourage each student to work for his or her personal best.

- Count the number of words read correctly in 30 seconds (words read minus errors).

  Multiply by two to determine words read correctly per minute. Record student scores.

b. Partner Reading

During students' daily independent work, have them do Partner Reading.

c. Homework 2

Have students read the story at home. (A reprint of this story is available on a blackline master in *Read Well* Homework.)

CHAPTER 2
See Miss Tam

What is the title of this chapter?[1] ("See Miss Tam")

Miss Tam was with the cat.

The cat wasn't mad.

That cat was sweet.

Miss Tam said, "I see that cat.

That cat can sit with me."

Miss Tam and the cat seem 😃 .

Why do you think they seem happy?[2]

FOCUS ON EXPRESSION

After students complete the first reading and before the second reading, have them practice three sentences at a time. Demonstrate expressive reading, guide expressive reading, then give individual turns.

40

❶ Identifying—Title

❷ Inferring

41

SENTENCE ILLUSTRATION

Use work pages from the workbook.

Identifying—Who
Describing

Writing
Identifying—Who

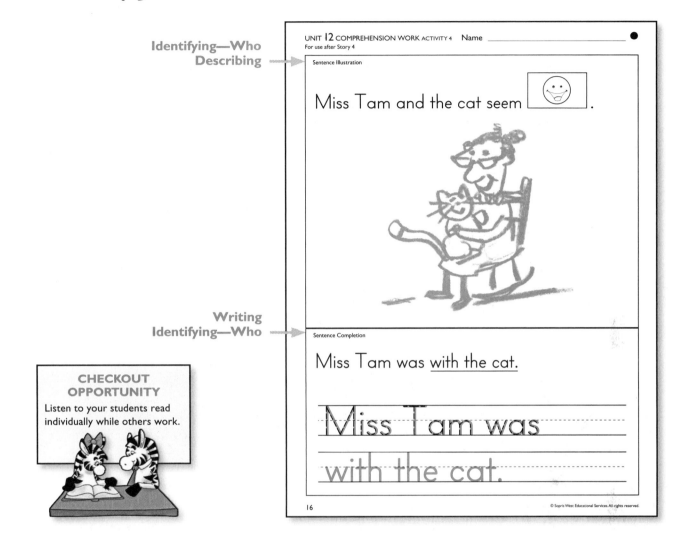

UNIT 12 COMPREHENSION WORK ACTIVITY 4   Name _____
For use after Story 4

Sentence Illustration

Miss Tam and the cat seem [☺].

Sentence Completion

Miss Tam was <u>with the cat.</u>

Miss Tam was
with the cat.

16

CHECKOUT OPPORTUNITY
Listen to your students read individually while others work.

PROCEDURES

For each step, demonstrate and guide practice as needed.

1. Sentence Illustration—Specific Instructions
- Have students read the sentence.
- Have students draw a picture of Miss Tam and the cat.

2. Sentence Completion—Specific Instructions
- Have students read the sentence.
- Have students identify the part of the sentence that they will complete.
- Have students trace and complete the sentence on the lines provided.

Note: Remind students that a sentence begins with a capital letter and ends with a period.

➊ SOUND REVIEW

➋ NEW SOUND PRACTICE

◆◆ **➌ STRETCH AND SHRINK**

Nat's-Nnnaaatsss-Nat's	That's *Nat's* [desk]. Whose [desk] is that? (*Nat's*)
hats-haaatsss-hats	How many *hats* do you have? (I have [two] *hats*.)
math-mmmaaathththth-math	After [reading], we do . . . (*math*).
with-wwwiiithththth-with	Who do you go to school *with*? (I go to school *with* [my friends].)

◆◆ **➍ SMOOTH AND BUMPY BLENDING—CARDS 25, 22**

◆◆ **➎ SOUNDING OUT SMOOTHLY**
- Have students say the underlined part, sound out the word, and then read the word. Use the words in sentences as needed.
- Repeat the row. Mix group and individual turns, independent of your voice.

✿ ***ssscaaat-scat***	The man said, "Go away! *Scat*!" What did he say? (*Scat*)
hiiid-hid	The dog *hid* under the bed.
wwweeeedzzz-weeds	What do you do with *weeds*? (Pull them.)

➏ ACCURACY AND FLUENCY BUILDING
- For each column, have students say the underlined part, then read the word.
- Have students read the whole column.
- Repeat practice on each column, building accuracy first and then fluency. (Remember, accuracy precedes rate. Make sure students are 100% accurate on a column; then use the column to build their response rate.)

◆◆ **➐ TRICKY WORDS**
★ **New word: "hasn't"**
- Have students find the small word "has" in their new Tricky Word. Then ask students to read the new word. (Tell students the word if needed.)
- Use "hasn't" in sentences.

  That hungry cat *hasn't* had his dinner.

  What is the cat's problem? (He *hasn't* had his dinner.)
- Repeat the row. Mix group and individual turns, independent of your voice.

➑ DAILY STORY READING
Proceed to the Unit 12 Storybook. See Daily Lesson Planning for pacing suggestions.

➒ COMPREHENSION AND SKILL WORK ACTIVITY 5 AND/OR ACTIVITY 6
See pages 45 and/or 50.

◆◆ For ELLs and children with language delays, provide repeated and extended practice with the language patterns. See page 10 for tips.

UNIT 12 DECODING PRACTICE 3
(For use with Stories 5 and 6)

1. SOUND REVIEW Use Sound Cards for Units 1–12 or Sound Review on Decoding Practice 4.

2. NEW SOUND PRACTICE Have students read the sound, then trace and say it.

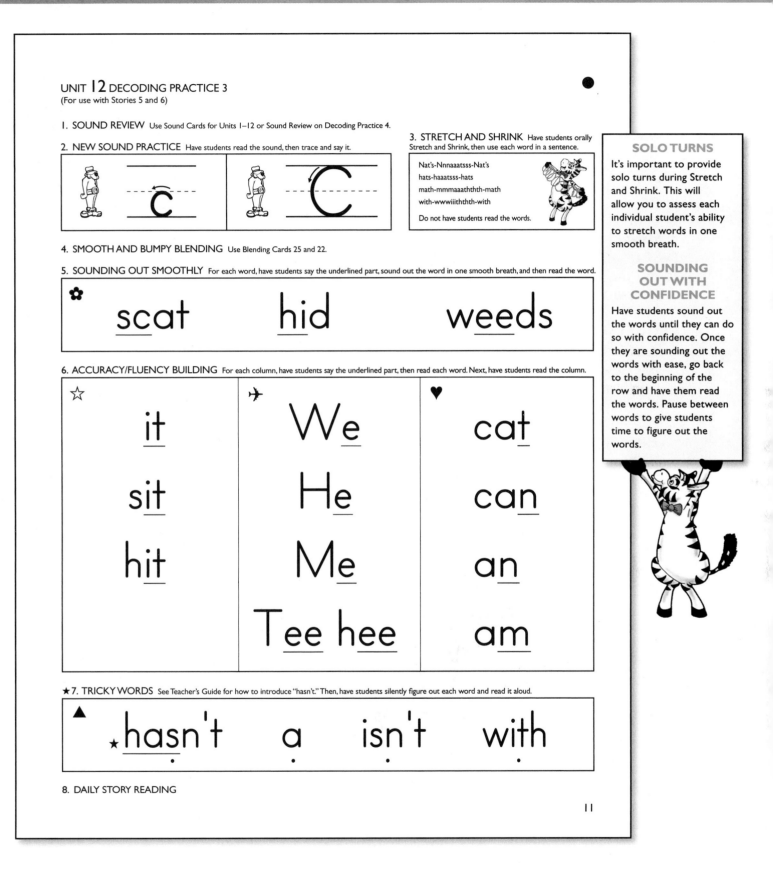

3. STRETCH AND SHRINK Have students orally Stretch and Shrink, then use each word in a sentence.

Nat's-Nnnaaatsss-Nat's
hats-haaatsss-hats
math-mmmaaaththth-math
with-wwwiiiththth-with

Do not have students read the words.

SOLO TURNS

It's important to provide solo turns during Stretch and Shrink. This will allow you to assess each individual student's ability to stretch words in one smooth breath.

SOUNDING OUT WITH CONFIDENCE

Have students sound out the words until they can do so with confidence. Once they are sounding out the words with ease, go back to the beginning of the row and have them read the words. Pause between words to give students time to figure out the words.

4. SMOOTH AND BUMPY BLENDING Use Blending Cards 25 and 22.

5. SOUNDING OUT SMOOTHLY For each word, have students say the underlined part, sound out the word in one smooth breath, and then read the word.

scat	hid	weeds

6. ACCURACY/FLUENCY BUILDING For each column, have students say the underlined part, then read each word. Next, have students read the column.

it	We	cat
sit	He	can
hit	Me	an
	Tee hee	am

★7. TRICKY WORDS See Teacher's Guide for how to introduce "hasn't." Then, have students silently figure out each word and read it aloud.

hasn't	a	isn't	with

8. DAILY STORY READING

11

39

DUET STORY READING INSTRUCTIONS

Students read from their own storybooks.
The teacher reads the small text and students read the large text.

PACING

- 2- to 4-Day Plans: Have students do the first reading
  of Duet Story 5.
  Then proceed to repeated readings of Solo Story 6.
- 6- to 10-Day Plans: Have students do the first *and*
  second readings.

COMPREHENSION BUILDING:
DISCUSSION QUESTIONS AND TEACHER THINK ALOUDS

Ask questions and discuss text on the first or second reading when
indicated in the storybook in light gray text.

PROCEDURES

1. First Reading

- Tell students they are going to read the next chapter about
  Miss Tam and the cat.
- Have students choral read the student text.

2. Second Reading

Have students take turns, with each student reading one line
of student text.

ECHO READING
(Reminder)
Periodically, repeat the text
with good expression and
phrasing to enhance meaning.

STORY 5, DUET

CHAPTER 3

Miss Tam and the Cat

Who do you think this chapter will be about?[1] (Miss Tam)
Who else is in the story?[2] (The cat)

Miss Tam was an old woman who lived in a big old house at the edge of town. At half past two, an old cat had appeared on her porch. Miss Tam took pity on the poor cat and let him rest in her lap. At half past five, the cat came back. Miss Tam took pity on the cat and shared her dinner with him.

See Miss Tam and the cat.

Miss Tam sat in her big armchair by the fire reading a book.

42

❶ **Predicting**
❷ **Identifying—Who**

At half past nine,

Miss Tam said, "That cat hasn't

budged and it is time for bed." In a small little voice,

Miss Tam said, "Scat, cat!"

Use a small little voice and say, "Scat, cat."[1] Do you think Miss Tam really wanted the cat to leave?[2] (No) I don't think so either. If she wanted the cat to go, she would have said it in a loud voice.[3]

The old cat opened one eye, but he didn't budge.

Miss Tam said, "That cat isn't moving."

Then Miss Tam shrugged her shoulders and toddled up to bed.
What do you think is going to happen with the cat and Miss Tam?[4]

43

❶ **Demonstrating**

❷ **Inferring**

❸ **Teacher Think Aloud—Explaining**

❹ **Predicting**

STORY 5, DUET

The next morning at half past seven, Miss Tam fixed herself breakfast.
Then she placed a bowl of eggs by her feet. With a thump, the old cat
jumped down from the mantle and began eating a fine meal. Soon the cat
was rubbing against Miss Tam's leg—as if to thank her.

Was the cat happy?**1** (Yes) Why?**2**

At noon, Miss Tam sat down to eat a tuna sandwich, and placed some tuna
in a bowl by her feet. The cat purred loudly. Was the cat happy?**3**(Yes) Why?**4**

At dinner time, Miss Tam shared a meatloaf with the cat.

Was the cat happy?**5**(Yes) Why?**6**

44

● **Inferring**

❷ **Inferring, Explaining**

❸ **Inferring**

❹ **Inferring, Explaining**

❺ **Inferring**

❻ **Inferring, Explaining**

That <u>cat</u> <u>was</u> soon a fat old cat.

<u>He</u> <u>wasn't</u> <u>sad.</u>

<u>He</u> <u>was</u>  .

Miss <u>Tam</u> <u>was</u> [☺] too.

How do you think the cat felt?**1** (Happy) Why?**2**
How did Miss Tam feel?**3** (Happy) Why?**4**
I liked this story because Miss Tam and the cat found that they could make each other happy.**5**
What did you think about the story?**6**

45

❶ **Inferring**

❷ **Inferring, Explaining**

❸ **Inferring**

❹ **Inferring, Explaining**

❺ **Teacher Think Aloud—Responding**

❻ **Responding**

HEARING SOUNDS

Use work pages from the workbook.

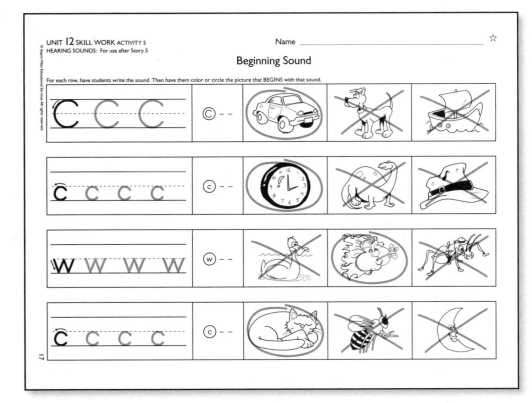

UNIT 12 SKILL WORK ACTIVITY 5
HEARING SOUNDS: For use after Story 5

Name _____

Beginning Sound

For each row, have students write the sound. Then have them color or circle the picture that BEGINS with that sound.

ANSWERS

Line 1: <u>car</u>, dog, boat
Line 2: <u>clock</u>, dinosaur, hat
Line 3: duck, <u>wind</u>, ant
Line 4: <u>cat</u>, bee, moon

PROCEDURES

Beginning Sound

Demonstrate and guide practice as needed.

- Have students write the beginning sound on the line.
- Have students color the picture word that begins with that sound.

Alternative: Have students write the beginning sound on the line, circle the picture word that begins with the sound, and cross out the picture words that do not begin with the sound.

PICTURE WORDS (Reminder)

Make sure that students know which sound they are looking for (beginning) and that they can identify the picture words prior to working independently.

SOLO STORY READING INSTRUCTIONS

Students read from their own storybooks.

COMPREHENSION BUILDING:
DISCUSSION QUESTIONS AND TEACHER THINK ALOUDS

Ask questions and discuss text on the first or second reading when indicated in the storybook in light gray text.

PROCEDURES

1. First Reading

- Explain to students that their Solo Story is the end, or conclusion, of "Miss Tam's Cat."
- Have students choral read the text.

2. Second Reading

- Mix group and individual turns, independent of your voice. Have students work toward an accuracy goal of 0–2 errors. Quietly keep track of errors made by all students in each group.
- After reading the story, practice any difficult words.
- If the group has not reached the accuracy goal, have the group reread the story, mixing group and individual turns.

3. Repeated Readings
a. Timed Readings

- Once the accuracy goal has been achieved, have individual students read the page while the other children track the text with their fingers and whisper read.

  Time individuals for 30 seconds and encourage each student to work for his or her personal best.

- Count the number of words read correctly in 30 seconds (words read minus errors). Multiply by two to determine words read correctly per minute. Record student scores.

b. Partner Reading

During students' daily independent work, have them do Partner Reading.

c. Homework 3

Have students read the story at home. (A reprint of this story is available on a blackline master in *Read Well* Homework.)

CHAPTER 4

Meet the 😄 Cat

What is the title of this chapter? ("Meet the Happy Cat")

"Tee hee," said Miss Tam.

"See the cat. That cat isn't sad.

That cat isn't mad. That cat is 😄.

"See the cat and me.

He can sit with me.

We can sit and sit."

46

❶ Identifying—Title

Look at the picture.

Who is the story about?[1] (Miss Tam and the cat)

Is the cat sad?[2] (No)

Is the cat mad?[3] (No)

The cat is . .[4] (happy).

Why do you think the cat is happy?[5]

47

❶ **Identifying—Who**

❷ **Inferring**

❸ **Inferring**

❹ **Inferring**

❺ **Inferring, Explaining**

COMPREHENSION BUILDING: ORAL STORY RETELL

- Have students study the pictures, then ask questions and discuss the pictures as indicated in the storybook in light gray text. The circle, square, and triangle provide visual references for the beginning, middle, and end of the story.

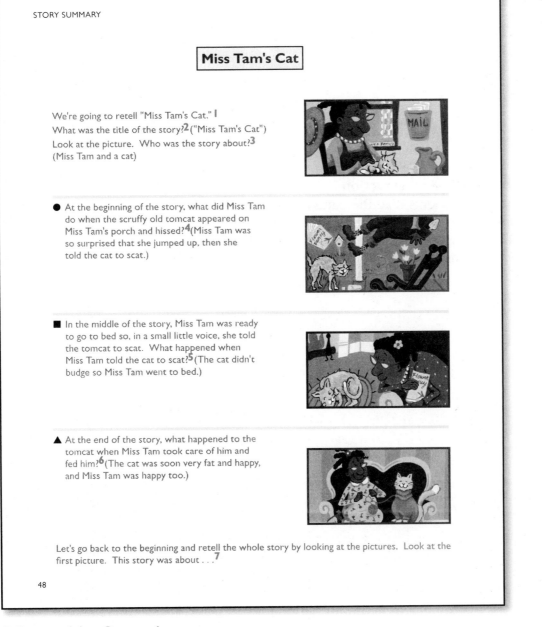

STORY SUMMARY

Miss Tam's Cat

We're going to retell "Miss Tam's Cat." **1**
What was the title of the story?**2** ("Miss Tam's Cat")
Look at the picture. Who was the story about?**3**
(Miss Tam and a cat)

● At the beginning of the story, what did Miss Tam do when the scruffy old tomcat appeared on Miss Tam's porch and hissed?**4** (Miss Tam was so surprised that she jumped up, then she told the cat to scat.)

■ In the middle of the story, Miss Tam was ready to go to bed so, in a small little voice, she told the tomcat to scat. What happened when Miss Tam told the cat to scat?**5** (The cat didn't budge so Miss Tam went to bed.)

▲ At the end of the story, what happened to the tomcat when Miss Tam took care of him and fed him?**6** (The cat was soon very fat and happy, and Miss Tam was happy too.)

Let's go back to the beginning and retell the whole story by looking at the pictures. Look at the first picture. This story was about . . .**7**

48

❶ **Summarizing, Sequencing**

❷ **Identifying—Title**

❸ **Identifying—Who**

❹ **Explaining—Beginning/Initiating Event**

❺ **Explaining—Middle**

❻ **Explaining—End**

❼ **Summarizing, Sequencing**

RHYMING PATTERNS

Use work pages from the workbook.

CHECKOUT OPPORTUNITY

Listen to your students read individually while others work.

PROCEDURES

Rhyming Patterns—Basic Instructions

- For each box, have students read the pattern at the top and then trace the letters and write the pattern on the lines to make words.
- Remind students to read the pattern words to themselves or to a partner when they finish the exercise.

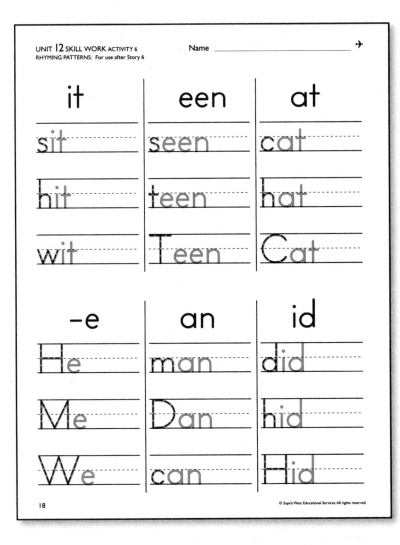

UNIT 12 SKILL WORK ACTIVITY 6
RHYMING PATTERNS: For use after Story 6

Name _____

it	een	at
sit	seen	cat
hit	teen	hat
wit	Teen	Cat

-e	an	id
He	man	did
Me	Dan	hid
We	can	Hid

18

Note: There are multiple uses for Decoding Practice 4.
- Use the Sound Review rows in place of Sound Card Practice.
- Use the whole page at the end of the unit for fluency building and/or to informally assess skills.
- Have students complete the page as a partner review.
- Build spelling dictation lessons from the sounds and words on this page.

❶ SOUND REVIEW

❷ ACCURACY AND FLUENCY BUILDING

The Airplane Columns are designed to help students build fluency with word patterns.
The Flower Columns are designed to help students make fine discriminations among words.
The primary focus is on accuracy.
Have students read each column, first for accuracy and then to build fluency.

❸ TRICKY WORDS

- Have students practice these rows until they can read all the words with 100% accuracy.
- Have them practice the words to increase their response rate.

❹ DAILY STORY READING

See Daily Lesson Planning for story suggestions.

EXTRA TRICKY WORD PRACTICE

- Write the following Tricky Words on the chalkboard: "I," "I'm," "said," "the," "was," "is," "his," "as," "has," "with," "a," "isn't," "wasn't," and "hasn't."

  Have students help you find small words in big words and identify words that rhyme.

- Keep a Tricky Word Wall going. If you haven't done so already, write the Tricky Words students have learned on cards and mount them on the wall. Change the order of the words at least once a week. Periodically, when there is a spare moment to fill, provide whole class practice. Mix group and individual turns during practice.

UNIT 12 DECODING PRACTICE 4
(See Daily Lesson Planning for story suggestions.)

1. SOUND REVIEW   Demonstrate an appropriate pace. Have students read the sounds in each row.

■	C	e	d	c	h	a	6
✿	t	W	c	i	th	m	12
♥	H	a	n	w	ee	C	18
●	i	c	s	h	C	e	24

2. ACCURACY/FLUENCY BUILDING   For each column, have students say the underlined part, then read each word. Next, have students read the column.

✈	✈ ✈	✈ ✈ ✈	✿	✿ ✿
H<u>at</u>s	s<u>ee</u>ds	m<u>iss</u>	<u>ant</u>	s<u>ee</u>n
C<u>at</u>s	h<u>ee</u>ds	Th<u>is</u>	<u>can</u>'t	t<u>ee</u>n
N<u>at</u>'s	w<u>ee</u>ds	Sw<u>iss</u>	<u>can</u>	t<u>in</u>
Th<u>at</u>'s	d<u>ee</u>ds	h<u>iss</u>	<u>cat</u>	w<u>in</u>

3. TRICKY WORDS   Have students silently figure out each word and then read it aloud.

☆☆	Wasn't said has the a	5
☆☆	isn't as with his hasn't	10

4. DAILY STORY READING

12

CULMINATING ACTIVITY

After students have practiced the skills on this page, play a blackout game. Identify a row or column. Read a word. As you count to three, have students find the word and cover it with a marker or square of paper.

End of the Unit

In this section, you will find:

Making Decisions

As you near the end of the unit, you will need to make decisions. Should you administer the Decoding Assessment or should you teach Extra Practice lessons?

Unit 12 Decoding Assessment

The Unit 12 Decoding Assessment is located on page 56 and can also be found in the *Assessment Manual*.

Certificate of Achievement and Goal Setting

Celebrate your children's accomplishments.

Extra Practice

Lessons and blackline masters for added decoding practice and independent work are provided for students who need extended practice opportunities.

Making Decisions

ASSESSMENT READINESS

Assess when students are able to easily complete decoding tasks from the beginning of a lesson.

- If you aren't sure whether students are ready for the assessment, give the assessment. Do Extra Practice lessons if needed.
- If students are not ready for the assessment, proceed to Extra Practice lessons. Administer the assessment as soon as students are ready.

GENERAL ASSESSMENT GUIDELINES

- Assess each child individually.
- Score student responses on the Student Assessment Record, adhering to the scoring criteria in the *Assessment Manual*. Use a stopwatch to time how long it takes the student to read Subtest D.
- Follow the general instructions at the bottom of each assessment. Record a Strong Pass, a Weak Pass, or a No Pass.

> ### SPECIAL SCORING INFORMATION
> #### Sounding Out Smoothly
> If a student reads the word without sounding out in Subtest B, give the student positive feedback, but check to see that the student can sound out the word. Say something like: You can read the word very easily. Now I'd like to see if you can sound it out slowly and smoothly—really stretch that word out.

ACCELERATION

- If students score 100% across all subtests and read Subtest D in less than 30 seconds, consider shortening units. Do not skip Unit 13.
- If an individual student scores 100% across all subtests and reads Subtest D significantly faster than other students in the group, assess the student for placement in the next higher group.

INTERVENTION OPTIONS—INDIVIDUALS

1. Add informal practice throughout the day.
2. Add practice with repeated readings on Solo Stories.
3. Find ways to provide a double dose of *Read Well* instruction.
    - Have the student work in his or her group *and* a lower group.
    - Have an instructional assistant, older student, or parent volunteer preview or review lessons.
    - Have an instructional assistant provide instruction with Extra Practice lessons.
4. Consider placement in a lower group. If one child's fluency scores are significantly lower than the other children in the group, success will be impossible without additional and intensive practice.

INTERVENTION OPTIONS—GROUP

1. Extend the unit with Extra Practice lessons.
2. Consider a Jell-Well Review before moving forward. (See page 9.)

CERTIFICATE OF ACHIEVEMENT AND GOAL SETTING

When students pass the assessment, celebrate with the Certificate of Achievement. Then, help children set personal goals. (See *Getting Started*.)

CRITICAL ASSESSMENT

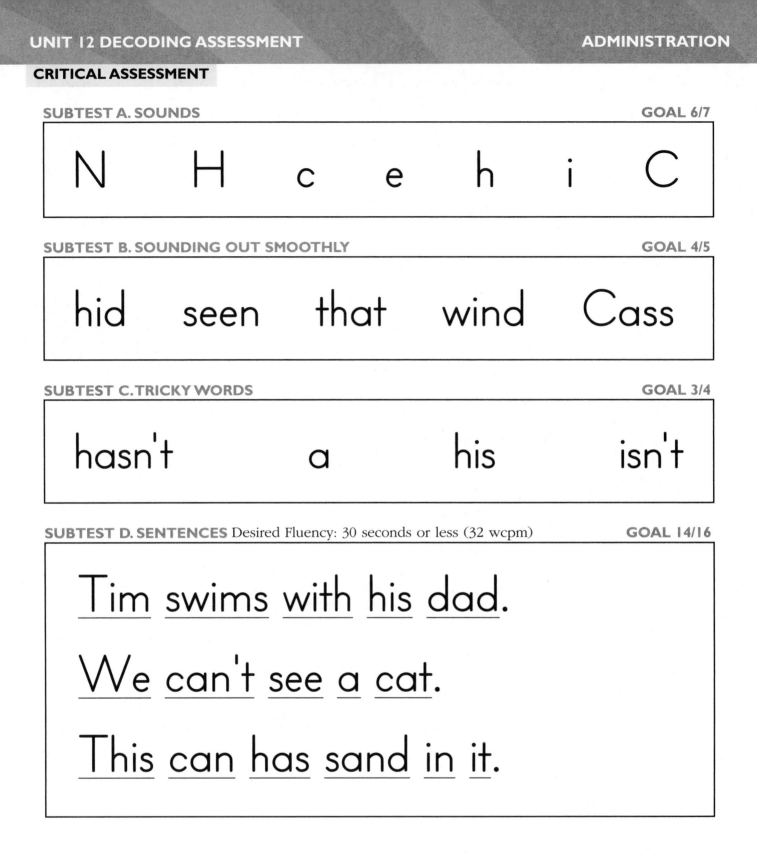

SUBTEST A. SOUNDS   GOAL 6/7

N   H   c   e   h   i   C

SUBTEST B. SOUNDING OUT SMOOTHLY   GOAL 4/5

hid   seen   that   wind   Cass

SUBTEST C. TRICKY WORDS   GOAL 3/4

hasn't   a   his   isn't

SUBTEST D. SENTENCES Desired Fluency: 30 seconds or less (32 wcpm)   GOAL 14/16

Tim swims with his dad.

We can't see a cat.

This can has sand in it.

SCORING	If the student needs assistance, the item is incorrect.
STRONG PASS	The student meets the goals on all subtests and has attained the desired fluency. Proceed to Unit 13.
WEAK PASS	The student meets the goals on 3 out of 4 subtests and/or fails to attain the desired fluency. Proceed to Unit 13 with added practice, or provide Extra Practice lessons in Unit 12, and/or provide a Jell-Well Review.
NO PASS	The student fails to meet the goal on 2 or more subtests. Provide Extra Practice lessons and retest, and/or provide a Jell-Well Review.

Certificate of Achievement

This certifies that

_____,

on this _____ day of _____, _____,

has successfully completed

Read Well Unit 12

Sounds Mastered: s, e, ee, m, a, d, th, n, t, w, i, Th, h, c

Words Mastered: I, see, I'm, me, am, Sam, mam, seem, sad, seed, mad, add, dad, said, seeds, seems, the, Nan, man, sees, Sams, an, and, than, seen, deed, sand, need, Dan, needs, at, sat, meet, meets, that, mat, ant, ants, was, Ann, we, weed, weeds, sweet, Nat, Dee, tan, in, it, sit, this, did, Tim, wind, that's, miss, win, mist, mints, tin, teen, sits, as, has, is, his, with, Dad's, dim, had, hand, hat, he, heed, hid, him, mint, mitt, Sam's, swim, swims, hasn't, isn't, wasn't, can, can't, Cass, cat, cat's, deeds, didn't, hadn't, hats, heeds, hiss, hit, miss, Nat's, scat, swiss, Tam, tee hee

Personal Goal Setting

I would like to be able to:

_____

I can work on my goal by:

_____

My teacher will tell me when he or she notices me working on my goal.

Date _____   Student Signature _____

Teacher Signature _____

◆◆ **❶ SMOOTH AND BUMPY BLENDING**
Select from Blending Cards 1–25 for review.

◆◆ **❷ STRETCH AND SHRINK**

can-caaannn-can	What *can* we do? (We *can* [read].)
cat-caaat-cat	What does a *cat* say? (A *cat* says "meow.")
hat-haaat-hat	See the cat and the . . . (*hat*).

❸ SOUND DICTATION
Have students write each sound, then check and correct.

/c/ at the beginning of "cat" with small letter <u>c</u>

/iii/ at the beginning of "insect" with small letter <u>i</u>

/h/ at the beginning of "hippo" with small letter <u>h</u>

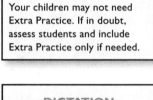

CAUTION
Your children may not need
Extra Practice. If in doubt,
assess students and include
Extra Practice only if needed.

◆◆ **❹ WORD DICTATION**
Have students count the sounds in each word with their fingers,
identify and write each sound, and then read the word.

can	What *can* we do? (We *can* [read].)
cat	What does a *cat* say? (A *cat* says "meow.")
hat	See the cat and the . . . (*hat*).

The first word is "can." What can we do? (We can [read].)
We're going to count the sounds in "can."
Tell me the first sound. **Hold up one finger.** (/c/)
Repeat with /aaa/ and /nnn/.
How many sounds are in "can"? (Three)

Tell me the first sound. (/c/) Write it.
Repeat with /aaa/ and /nnn/.
Do Smooth Blending. (/caaannn/) Read the word. (can)
What *can* we do? (We can [read].)

Repeat with "cat" and "hat."

DICTATION
• Demonstrate and guide
practice as needed.
• Have students check and
correct.

❺ POSSESSIVE '<u>S</u>
• Have students sound out each word, then read the phrase. (Remind students that they
sound out words with the apostrophe just like they sound out other words.)
• Repeat practice, mixing group and individual turns, independent of your voice.

❻ SOUNDING OUT SMOOTHLY

❼ TRICKY WORDS

❽ DAILY STORY READING
Proceed to Extra Practice Activity 1.
• Have students read each sentence from the book.
• Repeat, mixing group and individual turns, independent of your voice.

❾ EXTRA PRACTICE ACTIVITY I—CHECKOUT OPPORTUNITY
Have students fold, color, and read the book.

UNIT **12** EXTRA PRACTICE I   Name_____

1. SMOOTH AND BUMPY BLENDING Select from Blending Cards 1–25 for review.

2. STRETCH AND SHRINK Have students orally
Stretch and Shrink, then use each word in a sentence.

3. SOUND DICTATION Have students write each sound, then check and correct:
/c/ at the beginning of "cat," /iii/ at the beginning of "insect," /h/ at the beginning of "hippo."

```
can-caaannn-can
cat-caaat-cat
hat-haaat-hat
```

Do not have students read the words.

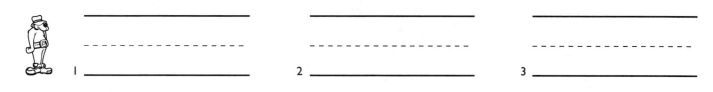

4. WORD DICTATION Have students count the sounds in each word, identify and write each sound, and then read the word: "can," "cat," and "hat."

1 _____   2 _____   3 _____

5. POSSESSIVE 'S Have students sound out each word, then read the phrase.

The cat's hat   Miss Tam's cat   The man's can

6. SOUNDING OUT SMOOTHLY For each word, have students sound out the word in one smooth breath, and then read the word.

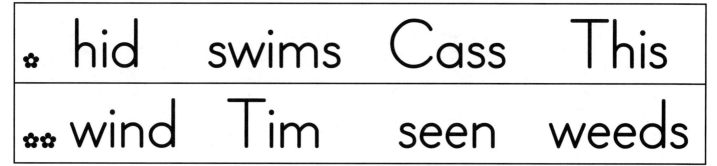

hid swims Cass This

wind Tim seen weeds

7. TRICKY WORDS For each word, have students silently figure out the word, then read it aloud.

with hasn't a said was

8. DAILY STORY READING

Blackline Master 59

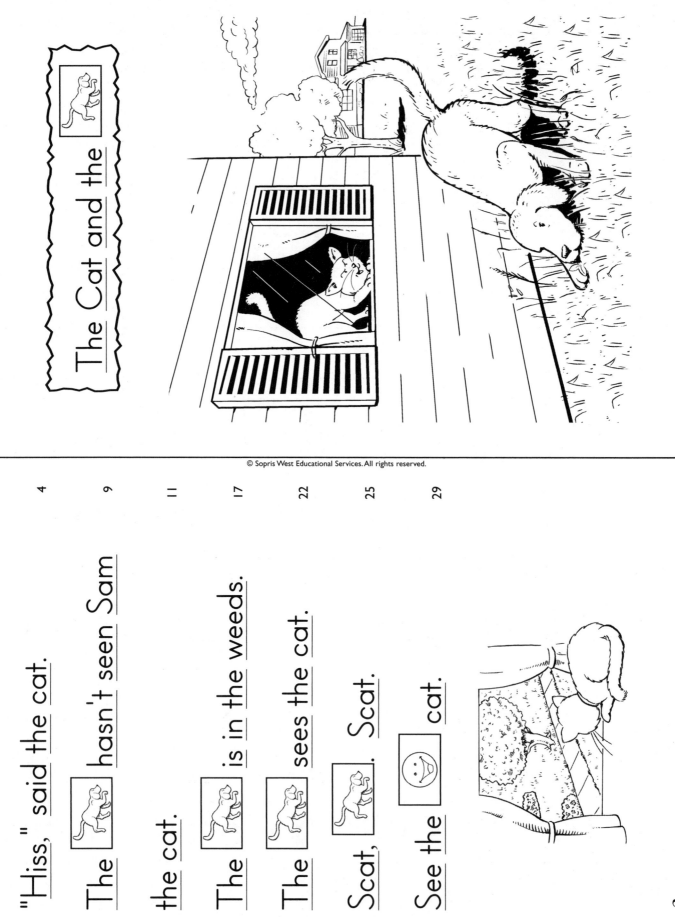

The Cat and the

4

9

11

17

22

25

29

"Hiss," said the cat.

The hasn't seen Sam

the cat.

The is in the weeds.

The sees the cat.

Scat, . Scat.

See the cat.

3

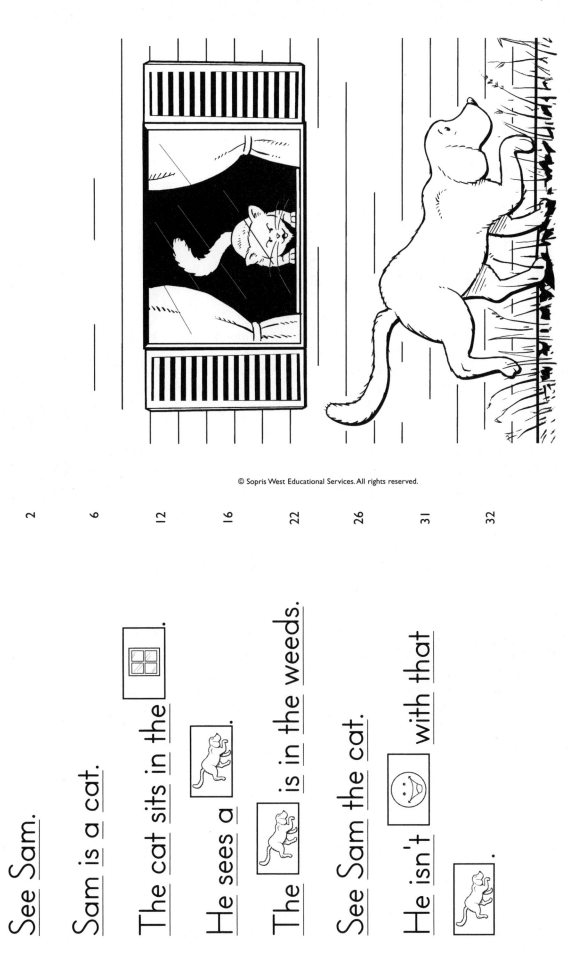

See Sam.

Sam is a cat.

The cat sits in the ___.

He sees a ___.

The ___ is in the weeds.

See Sam the cat.

He isn't ___ with that ___.

2

6

12

16

22

26

31

32

1

2

◆◆ 1 SMOOTH AND BUMPY BLENDING

Select from Blending Cards 1–25 for review.

◆◆ 2 STRETCH AND SHRINK

we-wwweee-we	*We* are [reading].What are *we* doing?
can-caaannn-can	What *can* we do? (We *can* [read].)
him-hiiimmm-him	Look at [Dillon]. See *him* [read].

3 SOUND DICTATION

Have students write each sound, then check and correct.

/iii/ at the beginning of "insect" with small letter <u>i</u>
/C/ at the beginning of "Cat" with capital letter <u>C</u>
/eee/ at the beginning of "emu" with small letter <u>e</u>

> **CAUTION**
>
> Your children may not need Extra Practice. If in doubt, assess students and include Extra Practice only if needed.

◆◆ 4 WORD DICTATION

Have students count the sounds in each word with their fingers, identify and write each sound, and then read the word.

We	*We* are [reading]. What are *we* doing?
Can	*Can* we [read]? (Yes, we *can* [read].)
him	Look at [Dillon]. See *him* [read].

HAVE STUDENTS CHECK AND CORRECT.

The first word is "We." We are [reading].What are we doing?
We're going to count the sounds in "We."
Tell me the first sound. **Hold up one finger.** (/WWW/)
Tell me the next sound. **Hold up two fingers.** (/eee/)
How many sounds are in "We"? (Two)

Tell me the first sound. (/WWW/) Write it with a capital <u>W</u>.
Tell me the next sound. (/eee/) Write it.
Do Smooth Blending. (/Wwweee/) Read the word. (We)
We are [reading].What are we doing?

Repeat with "Can" and "him."

5 ACCURACY/FLUENCY BUILDING

• For each column, have students say any underlined part, then read the word.
• Have students read the whole column.
• Repeat practice on each column, building accuracy first and then fluency.

6 TRICKY WORDS

Repeat practice, mixing group and individual turns, independent of your voice.

7 DAILY STORY READING

Proceed to Extra Practice Activity 2.
• Have students read each sentence.
• Repeat, mixing group and individual turns, independent of your voice.

8 EXTRA PRACTICE ACTIVITY 2—CHECKOUT OPPORTUNITY

As you listen to individuals read the story, have students color the picture.

◆◆ For ELLs and children with language delays, provide repeated and extended practice with the language patterns. See page 10 for tips.

1. SMOOTH AND BUMPY BLENDING Select from Blending Cards 1–25 for review.

2. STRETCH AND SHRINK Have students orally Stretch and Shrink, then use each word in a sentence.

3. SOUND DICTATION Have students write each sound, then check and correct: /iii/ at the beginning of "insect," /C/ at the beginning of "Cat," /eee/ at the beginning of "emu."

we-wwweee-we
can-caaannn-can
him-hiiimmm-him

Do not have students read the words.

4. WORD DICTATION Have students count the sounds in each word, identify and write each sound, and then read the word: "We," "Can," and "him."

1 _____   2 _____   3 _____

5. ACCURACY/FLUENCY BUILDING In each column, have students say any underlined part, then read each word. Next, have students read the column.

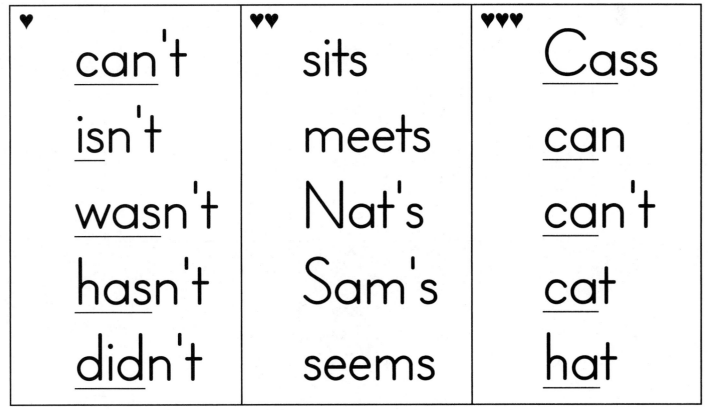

♥	♥♥	♥♥♥
<u>can</u>'t	sits	<u>Cass</u>
<u>isn</u>'t	meets	can
<u>wasn</u>'t	Nat's	<u>can</u>'t
<u>hasn</u>'t	Sam's	<u>cat</u>
<u>didn</u>'t	seems	<u>hat</u>

6. TRICKY WORDS For each word, have students silently figure out the word, then read it aloud.

a   his   was   The   with

7. DAILY STORY READING

Name_____

Note: Have students identify the picture words "house" and "sad" before they read.

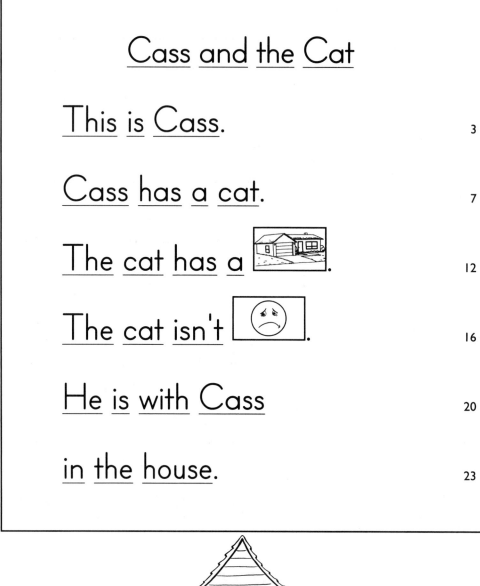

Cass and the Cat

This is Cass.   3

Cass has a cat.   7

The cat has a .   12

The cat isn't [😞].   16

He is with Cass   20

in the house.   23

Have students read the sentences. Time individual students for 30 seconds; mark errors. To determine words correct per minute (wcpm), count words read in 30 seconds, subtract errors, multiply times two, and record on the chart for the first reading. (Repeated readings may be completed with older students, assistants, or parents.)

My goal is to read with 0–2 errors. This is what I did:

Reading	1st	2nd	3rd	4th
Errors				
Words/ 30 seconds				
wcpm				

① **STORYBOOK DECODING REVIEW**

For each row, mix group and individual turns, independent of your voice.

② **SOLO STORY REVIEW—
UNITS 9 AND 10**

- Guide student reading, gradually increasing rate.
- Mix group and individual turns on the stories, independent of your voice.
- Repeat practice. While one student reads, have others track the text with their fingers and whisper read.

> **CAUTION**
>
> Your children may not need Extra Practice 3 and 4. If in doubt, assess students and include Extra Practice only if needed.

③ **EXTRA PRACTICE ACTIVITY 3—CHECKOUT OPPORTUNITY**

- Have students cut out the Letter Cards and arrange them on the Letter Card Grid to create the words "can," "cat," "hat," "hid," "had," "him," "tan," and "tin" in the blank row at the top of the page.
- Have students arrange and glue the letters in the remaining rows to create "can," "cat," and "hat." (While students are gluing letters, listen to individuals read a Solo Story.)

Challenge Activity: With the remaining letters, have students make a word in the blank row.

① **DECODING PRACTICE 4 REVIEW**

For each row, mix group and individual turns, independent of your voice.

② **SOLO STORY REVIEW—UNITS 11 AND 12**

- Guide student reading, gradually increasing rate and emphasizing expression.
- Mix group and individual turns on the stories, independent of your voice.
- Repeat practice. (While one student reads, have others track the text with their fingers and whisper read.)

③ **EXTRA PRACTICE ACTIVITY 4—CHECKOUT OPPORTUNITY**

- Have students cut out the Memory Cards. (While students are cutting out their cards, listen to individuals read a Solo Story.)
- Once the cards have been cut out, have the group or pairs of students play Memory.
  Using one set of cards, spread the cards out in rows with the words facing down.
  Have students take turns. Each time a card is turned over, have the group or pair identify the word.
  If the words match, have students set the pair off to the side.
  If the words do not match, have students turn the cards back over and try again.

Letter Cards

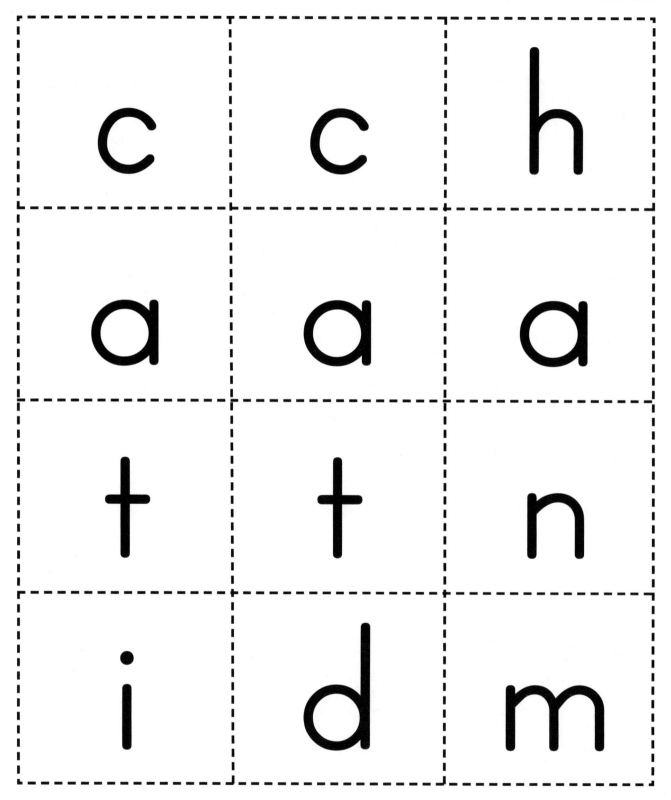

Name_____

Letter Card Grid

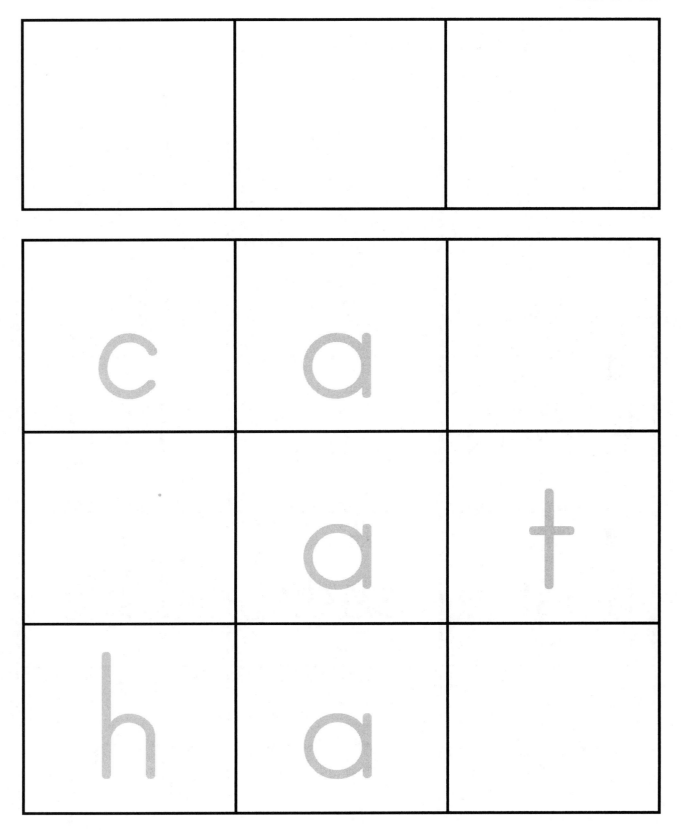

Memory Cards

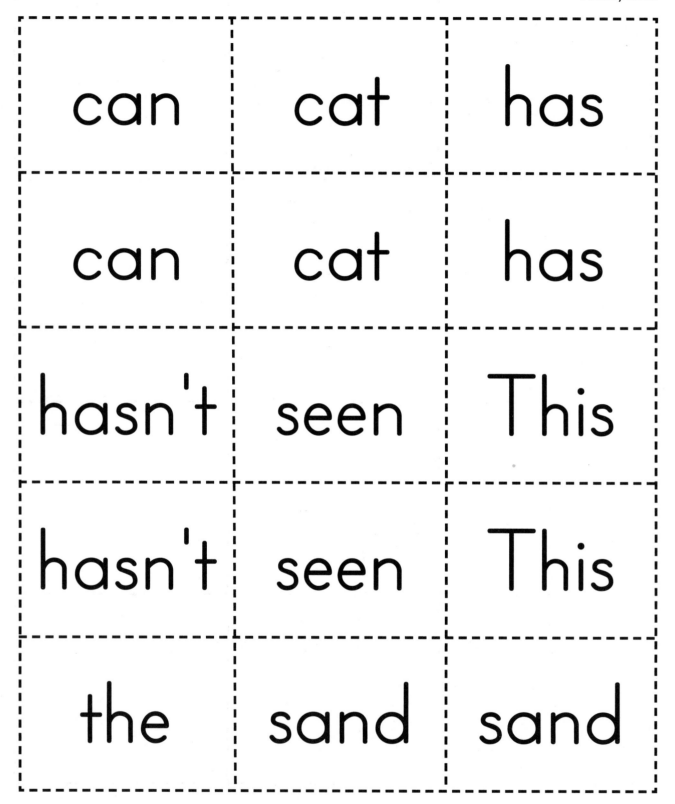

can	cat	has
can	cat	has
hasn't	seen	This
hasn't	seen	This
the	sand	sand

Note: The Memory Cards can also be used to create sentences. Also, note there is no match for the word "the."